C. Mills

Lincoln Christian College

SUDDENLY Single

JIM SMOKE

SUDDENLY Single

Fleming H. Revell Company
Old Tappan, New Jersey

Unless otherwise identified, Scripture quotations are from the Revised Standard Version of the Bible, copyrighted 1946, 1952, © 1971 and 1973.
Scripture quotations identified KJV are from the King James Version of the Bible.
Scripture quotations identified PHILLIPS are from THE NEW TESTA-MENT IN MODERN ENGLISH (Revised Edition), translated by J. B. Phillips. © J. B. Phillips 1958, 1960, 1972. Used by permission of Macmillan Publishing Co., Inc.
Quotation from the poem "Ambivalence" is by Nancy D. Potts, *Beginning Again: The Challenge of the Formerly Married.*
Quotation from "The 59th Street Bridge Song" © 1966, 1967 Paul Simon. Used by permission.
Diligent effort has been made to secure permission for all quotations used in this book.

Library of Congress Cataloging in Publication Data

Smoke, Jim.
    Suddenly single.

    Bibliography: p.
    1. Single people—Religious life. I. Title.
BV4596.S5S63   248.8'4   82-629
ISBN 0-8007-1312-5   AACR2

TO Carol
Wife and Friend

Special thanks to the many single adults all across America who are my friends

To Fritz Ridenour, editor and friend

To Kathy Guzman, typist and affirmer

To Priscilla Edwards, secretary and affirmer

To Janet Warner, associate editor

Contents

Preface

This book is about a journey, one well known to millions of "suddenly single" adults. It is a collection of conversations overheard as I have traveled across America. It contains the questions, fears, dreams, frustrations, doubts, and optimism of men and women who are single again because of death or divorce. They are all a part of this book and the experiences I have shared.

This is not, however, a book about the crisis of going through death and divorce. There are many good books that deal with this. It is about what happens well after the ink has dried on divorce decrees and death certificates. It is about picking up the pieces and putting a life back together. I offer an affirmative answer to the question "Is there life after the death or divorce of a spouse?"

Of the 53 million single adults in our country, many are divorced or widowed. Some of their frustrations are summed up in the words of one lady who stopped me after a singles conference and said, "I've been divorced for three years. I am well past the crisis. I don't know who I am anymore and even worse, I don't know what I will become."

Honestly, practically, and simply, I hope to shed some light on statements like this and questions you might have as you read this book.

JIM SMOKE

1

In Transition or Out of Commission

As I speak to and counsel thousands of single adults each year, one word seems to come to the surface in every conversation. The word is *transition*. The dictionary says transition means "a passage from one place, condition, or action to another; change."

Becoming suddenly single again by the death or divorce of a mate brings a person face to face with changes he or she had not planned for or desired as a part of his life's journey. The plans, in fact, were to live happily ever after. The wedding ceremony seemed to guarantee it. But there are no guarantees!

There are two basic struggles in becoming single again. The first deals with the immediate crisis of loss and the acceptance and resolution of it. For most people, in both death and divorce, that initial process takes two to three years. The second struggle which we will deal with in this book is about facing the challenges in rebuilding a life.

How Do You Know Where You Are Right Now?

I speak with many single-again people who ask me to help them pinpoint where they are in their struggle. They need to know where they are right now and where they are headed. Is the crisis over and the rebuilding beginning? Some people I meet have chosen to continually live at the crossroads of their crisis. Let me share several guidelines with you that will help you evaluate where you are right now.

1. Do you constantly talk about your former spouse to everyone?
2. Do you repeatedly tell your divorce or death story to everyone?
3. Do you feel sorry for yourself most of the time?
4. Do you often play make-believe games in your mind?
5. Do you blame your former spouse for your present condition?
6. Do you feel that life has dealt you a cruel, unfair blow?
7. Do you tend to live more in the past than the present?

If you answered yes to one or more of these questions, you may still be struggling with your crisis. You cannot begin your rebuilding process as long as you are caught on the crisis side.

The Three Stages of Rebuilding

There are three stages most people have to work through as they rebuild their lives as single-again men and women.

The first stage involves looking back on the yesterday of your life and saying, "If I'd only. . . ." You don't have to think too long or too hard to come up with an immediate list of things you wish you had done differently. The truth is that you cannot change history or memories. You can only learn from them. Looking back with regret only dulls your hope for today.

In my work, I often refer to what the Bible tells us about situations we may face. The Apostle Paul said, "... forgetting what lies behind and straining forward to what lies ahead, I press on toward the goal for the prize of the upward call of God in Christ Jesus" (Philippians 3:13, 14). Paul had some things in his yesterdays that he wanted to forget. He knew that the only way this could happen was to live today, with his eyes open toward tomorrow.

Thinking in reverse only keeps you from moving forward. Many single-again people are still living in yesterday. Put all your yesterdays in your file drawer and concentrate on building today.

A second stage in rebuilding is known as forward-fear projection. It simply means you look at tomorrow and say to yourself, "What if ...?" What if you run out of money? What if you never remarry? What if you get sick and have no one to look after you? What if the stock market crashes and the gasoline supply dries up? What if your children become delinquents? The list could go on and on.

Fear of the future can immobilize you in the present and keep you from making the plans that will help you rebuild your life. Your future is a trust that is best handled by placing it in God's hands. Writing to the Early Christians at Philippi, Paul said, "Don't worry over anything whatever ... tell God every detail of your needs in thankful prayer ..." (Philippians 4:6 PHILLIPS).

The future can be frightening, not just for those who are

single again but for all of us. Only God can translate that fear into trust.

The third stage deals with living in the present. At the conclusion of a divorce-recovery workshop, a lady presented me with a gift. When I opened it, I found it was a blue T-shirt with the words I CAN DO emblazoned across the front in large, bold letters. Those words translate what living in the present is all about. They stand in direct contrast to the first two attitudes. They plant you in the present with the challenge to accept responsibility for your life and to start your renewal.

The *I can do*s usually start with small things: small plans, small challenges, small triumphs. As these build in your life, you begin to feel good about yourself and your progress. A man in a workshop recently summed it up. He said, "The road back is full of potholes and mountains. It is definitely more fun climbing mountains than falling into potholes."

Paul's *I can do* statement is found in Philippians 4:13. He said, "I can do all things in him who strengthens me." Paul was a rebuilder. He was a "right now" liver infused with God's strength.

What are your *I can do*s? Have you taken time lately to write them down? Are you saying, "I can go back to school; find a new career; do a good job of single parenting; be responsible for myself; rebuild and go on with my life"?

No one else can do your rebuilding for you. Sometimes the temptation is to go hunting for that special someone who can do the work for you or who already has a game plan going in his or her own life. If you were a dependent person in your past marriage, the tendency will be to search for a person who will continue to do everything for you. Many second marriages are started on this premise, and many of them fail. Healthy marriages are ones in which an interdependent relationship exists.

Transition Means Change

How comfortable do you feel with change? Most of us feel pretty nervous and uncertain about it. Reentry into the world of single-again adults is littered with uncertainties. It means leaving the married world behind and entering the singles world. This can be intimidating, considering all the negative things you might have read and heard about the singles scene. It's a new world. It means change. You cannot return to yesterday. You have to move ahead, even though you would like to run and hide.

In John's Gospel, there is an account in chapter 5 that demonstrates how radical change can be. Jesus singled out a man by the pool of Bethesda who had been ill for thirty-eight years. He asked the man a very strange yet probing question: "Do you want to get well again?" (John 5:6 PHIL-LIPS).

If someone had asked you that the last time you had the flu, you know what your answer would have been. Yet this man didn't seem to understand the question. Instead of a loud *yes,* he told Jesus that He didn't understand his problem. In response to that, Jesus instantly healed the man and sent him on his way to a new life. Perhaps the real question Jesus was asking was, "Do you want to make sweeping changes in your life?" Going from chronic sickness to total health would be a big change in anyone's life. Jesus seemed to know that there was to be a cost involved when the change took place. As I think about this incident, several aspects of the cost of change come to mind.

The first costly change to the man by the pool was giving up what was comfortably familiar. To all who used the pool, he seemed a permanent fixture. He had an identity, even though it was connected to his illness. He belonged and he was a familiar sight. But in order to get well, in order to change, he had to leave this familiar setting. And that had to be frightening.

Second, he had to give up whatever form of security he had found in his poolside residency and sickness. He knew the people by the pool. He knew the healing process. That gave him a sense of security. Sometimes even sickness can be a security blanket that keeps us from changing. We can pull our bad situation or unfair circumstance around us and use it as a shield against any new adventures and growth. Security can come in many different forms. Are you afraid to let go in order to make some gains?

On a third level, this man had to move into a situation he knew little about. Lack of knowledge can be a justifiable fear. But that fear is removed when we do our homework and start exploring. The man by the pool had been sick so long that being well was strange territory. For many single-again people, being married for any length of time makes being single again a very uncomfortable and unfamiliar place. It can seem as though a cruel trick has been played on you. The time machine has thrust you backward to your late teens or early twenties. The only difference is that you no longer look twenty-one.

In the Old Testament, God called Moses out of his semi-retirement life-style of minding the flocks of his father-in-law, Jethro. In the burning-bush conversation between God and Moses, Moses expressed his fear about leading the Israelites out of their bondage. God's promise to Moses was that He would go with him back into Egypt and give him the words to speak and the ability to be a leader. Moses went, not without a little fear and concern. But he went, and God's promise was fulfilled.

Singleness for the formerly married is a mystifying land. When you left singleness for marriage, you never expected to return. Moses never planned to go back to Egypt. He left for good, or so he thought. Going back could only be accomplished with the help of God. Asking for God's help in this single-again land can give you a new sense of direction and confidence.

The fourth area of change the man by the pool faced was risking the discovery of who he really was. For thirty-eight years he lived with one identity. Now all that was to be changed. Who would he be in his new role? Would he be accepted, loved, understood? Would people think well of him?

Self-discovery usually comes from the inside out. As outward conditions change, we reach inside ourselves to discover who we really are. One thing is certain: All of us are changing. We are caught in the process of becoming. So was the man by the pool.

Many single-again people wonder who they are. Some have told me they have no identity in singleness and can't wait to remarry. But identity does not come in duets. As a single-again person, you are changing and getting in touch with yourself. Things are no longer as they once were. You are discovering yourself.

The fifth confrontation with change for the man by the pool was facing rejection. I am sure that his new state of wholeness drew many reactions from those around him. His compatriots by the pool were perhaps so envious of his new life and so jealous of him that they no longer wanted his friendship. Skepticism about the healing encounter the man had could also have turned some healthy people away from him. Instead of celebrating his healing, they questioned it. Instead of affirming him, they withdrew. He could easily be a man caught between two worlds and rejected by both. Many single-again people can identify with this feeling. When you are going through changes, you seem to make those around you very nervous. It is sometimes easier for people to avoid you than to affirm you. It may make you want to escape the rejection via the route of a quick, new, instant relationship that leads in a few months to the altar of marriage.

Divorced people often have a strong sense of rejection. If your mate has left you for another person, rejection, self-doubt, and a lack of self-esteem all seem to stifle any attempts at rebuilding your life.

Even the typical singles community can send out waves of rejection to the person trying to enter it. Once entered, individual rejection can be encountered in the form of the dating, mating, relating process. It is little wonder that many choose to hide rather than to reach out.

Few of us, single or married, ever learn how to handle rejection with any amount of finesse. We bruise easily and we bleed freely. We heal slowly and move ahead warily.

The last area that the man by the pool had to deal with was changing his life-style. His old one was gone with a few words spoken by Jesus. His new one was to be an adventure that he had to embark upon whether or not he wanted to. He could not be well and stay in residence by the pool. He was forcibly thrust into a new way of living.

Much has been written about the single life-style. Depending upon where you do your reading, it may be summed up by "swinging singles," "headhunters in a land of search and seizure," "the invasion of the body snatchers," "losers and misfits," and "loners and lepers."

The truth is that single-again people are just plain people. Changing one's married status in life does not change the person into some two-headed monster. The thousands of singles I meet across America are simply looking for a pathway through singleness. They are trying to accept it as a part of life rather than a rough spot between marriages or a place to simply stagnate until rescued.

One of the big helps in living through singleness, whether for life or a few years, is found in Paul's letter to the Philippians. From his prison cell he said, ". . . I have learned to be content, whatever the circumstances may be" (Philippians 4:11 PHILLIPS). Paul had many things going for him. His life was exciting. But at the height of everything, he was thrown in jail. He had it all and lost it. However, Paul's secret of living was trusting Christ in all situations. The presence of Christ filled every nook and cranny that Paul found himself in. He never suffered from "situation vacillation." He learned to trust God and rest in the process.

By now, you may have found yourself comparing your life changes to those of the man by the pool of Bethesda. He was introduced to a new life. You were, also. He did not have a choice. Perhaps neither did you. His fears and challenges were equally divided. So are yours.

Where are you as you face the changes that sudden singleness has brought your way? You may have moved beyond your crisis, but are you moving down the road of growth? I want to share four questions with you that will help you further evaluate your status and help you get a grip on the handle of growth. Don't just read them and go on. Spend some time with them. They demand some homework. Think carefully about each one.

1. *Where am I now?* This is an evaluation question. If you don't know where you are, you won't know where you are going. Some of the key areas that demand evaluation are mental, physical, emotional, spiritual, vocational, practical, and social.

Are you making progress in the above areas? Are you stalled in some while moving in others? What are your growth priorities in each area? After you make a list of where you feel you are in each area, make a second list, planning out where you want to be and what it will take to get there. Before you start asking others for their opinions, write your own down first. Start from the feeling level and be honest.

2. *Who am I now?* This is an identification question. The tendency here is to answer this by telling who you were rather than who you are. Right now, who you are is more important than who you were. In the Scriptures, God sometimes gave His servants a new name. The new name often described the kind of person they had become. Their challenge was to live up to the new name and build a new identity.

"Who am I now?" is a question of feeling and exploration. It is a question about building and expanding a little each day. Sometimes that growth is best expressed in being able to say out loud, "I am single." These are difficult words for divorced and widowed people to say. It is much easier to say, "I am widowed" or "I am divorced" than to say, "I am single."

Hanging like a rainbow over all you think you are is what God knows you are. That is the knowledge that you are loved by Him.

3. *Where do I go from here?* This is known as a direction question. I am always asking directions when I travel. I usually want to know the quickest and easiest route to my destination. Some people neglect to tell me that my route sometimes contains detours. Detours take time and are seldom enjoyable. They are definitely inconvenient. But they are a part of the journey.

Sudden singleness can seem like an eternal detour, but only if you choose to park by the sign. Getting directions means making plans and having goals. Others can sometimes point you in the right direction, but you have to take the journey.

4. *How do I get there?* I call this an achievement question. It has to do with the vehicle for travel. A street-wise young man in New York was asked the directions to Carnegie Hall. His response was, "Practice, man, practice." No one else can do your practicing for you. Many single-again people have no destination and no means of getting anywhere.

In my ten years of working with single people, some of the happiest times have been listening to the stories of goals reached and achievements accomplished. In divorce-recovery workshops, I often meet people at the crisis point in their lives. Their most important concern at that moment seems to be to continue breathing. What a serendipity to meet them a year or two later and share in their progress and victories. I hear them say, "I went back to school."

"I got that job."

"I moved and bought my own house."

"I joined a good singles group."

"I am making it on my own."

Are you in transition or completely out of commission? Being caught in the middle is never the most comfortable place. At certain times, you will feel like not much is coming together for you. This is normal because changes don't always follow predictable patterns. The desire of most of us is to "have it all together." Somehow that would prove to the rest of the world that we are okay. Some of us would readily identify with the little sign that says, I'VE GOT IT ALL TO- GETHER, BUT I FORGET WHERE I PUT IT.

Getting it together is a lifelong process. Making changes is a part of that process. Look at your options and opportunities as you make your decisions. Don't hide behind your fears.

Life is like driving on the freeway. You are always changing lanes. Changing lanes in your life often means rediscovering who you are in a situation where fear and adventure are new traveling companions.

Personal-Growth Questions

(For best results, work with a small group
or one other person.)

1. Write down your three biggest *If I'd only*s.
2. Share your three biggest *What if*s.
3. Name three things you *can do* that will help you grow personally.
4. What are two of the biggest changes that happened in your life over the past year?
5. Of the six changes that took place in the life of the man Jesus healed, with which one do you identify the most and why?

2

I Don't Know Who I Am

Moving from the world of the married to the world of the suddenly single again can cause an identity crisis. The world of the married can offer a cocoon of security to you. It means belonging to someone special and to the community called marriage. It is being surrounded by people who affirm that you belong there. Suddenly, that world collapses and you are ejected into a world that seems to belong to another galaxy.

A basic fear that many single-again persons face is the fear of having to start all over again after they have accumulated twenty or thirty years of marital experience. Starting over in this sense can mean many things. The most fearful seems to be relating to members of the opposite sex through dating. As one lady described it: "The only difference between being single at forty-five and single at eighteen is that at forty-five, you aren't fighting pimples any longer." The thought of having a second adolescence is not too comforting. Going through it once was enough.

Building a new identity as a single-again person raises

many questions and provides too few replies. I want to ask some of those questions and try to offer helpful answers.

Why Am I Afraid of the Word *Single?*

The word *single* is fine for a person under twenty-five years old. Above that, it can signify failure to the bearer and to others in his or her life. Society still seems to feel that people come in pairs. Those who are paired feel most at ease around others who are paired. If you are a never-married single over twenty-five, speculation as to why you are still single is open to widespread discussion. The "how come" seems to come up daily.

If the word *single* is a problem to the never married, it is even more of a problem to the formerly married. The "how come" is replaced by the "I wonder what happened." You spend hours planning a six-page answer to that so you can respond when asked. You will want to say that you are single but you are not like all those "other" single-again people out there. You and your situation are different from the other 53 million. We could say that this is called "wanting an identity but not wanting to identify with others."

I meet many singles who steadfastly refuse to attend any singles group or singles function. I know of a church that has over eight hundred singles on its rolls, yet less than a third of that number are involved in its singles ministry. Sometimes a bad first experience in a singles group sends one packing. Perhaps you have conjured up your own somewhat distorted ideas of who other singles are and how they feel. Have you given them a chance? Better still, have you given yourself a chance with them? Clinging desperately to a married mentality will not help you accept your new singleness.

Singleness is simply a part of your journey through life, much as childhood and adolescence were. It is a place of change and transition, as I said in chapter 1. You need to know that it is all right to be there. Singleness is not a disease cured by death or marriage. It is not meant to be a holding pattern during your trip through life.

Many singles have shared their feelings about singleness with me. The ones who are really growing and dealing with their single identity are the ones who can say, "It's not where I meant to be in my life, and it's not where I want to be, but I accept it and will use it as a place to grow."

Don't be afraid of the word *single*. It is not synonymous with failure, and it's not contagious. Don't let others put you into an identity box because of what their image of singleness is. Singleness is not a place to hide until someone discovers you and spirits you away to the marriage altar. It is your place to live and grow right now.

Do I Have to Spend All My Singleness With Single People?

I certainly hope not. I hear a lot of arguments about single people being isolated from other groups, particularly in church life. Singles groups, fellowships, and socials are not an attempt to herd all single people together in an isolation ward. They are honest attempts to meet needs and provide a place for fellowship and growth. Friendships need to be made with fellow strugglers. There will always be special times for inclusion with other groups and for exclusion with your own group. Both are important in the single person's life.

It is human nature to move with the people who are interested in the things we are interested in. They become our close friends due to mutual interests. Single-again people who are ready to build new and meaningful relationships want to spend time with other singles. Find the level of balance in this area for yourself and begin to reach out and touch others.

What If I Never Remarry?

An attractive and poised lady in her late fifties approached me at the end of a singles conference. She led me over to a quiet corner of the room and asked a question I have heard hundreds of times before: "Where are all the good men my age?"

Sometimes I jokingly reply, "Anchorage, Alaska, the last frontier." Once in a while, a woman is willing to move to Alaska. It's a question to which there are no easy answers.

A single-again person under the age of thirty-five doesn't seem to worry as much about finding someone to remarry as a person over forty or fifty. The field of likely candidates narrows dramatically as your age climbs. There are several reasons.

First, many men in their fifties want to date and relate to women in their thirties or forties. Whether or not you say this is an ego problem is unimportant. The fact is that it's a social reality. Even your thought that it's not fair doesn't help the problem. It simply exists.

Second, men over fifty tend to die off more rapidly than women.

Third, men seem to find it more difficult to join social groups than women. Women tend to be more relational, while men are more vocational and occupational.

A fourth reason is that our society says a man can initiate a relationship with a woman, but a woman must sit and wait until asked by a man. When a man has a lot of choices, a woman may find herself spending a lot of time on the bench waiting to be invited into the game.

The reality in all of this is that many men and women who have lost a mate by death or divorce will never remarry. That can sound like a very negative and lonely statement, but facing and dealing with reality is more growth producing than living in a fantasy. This is why the building of all levels of relationships is so important to the single person. Those relationships are not intended to take the place of your former spouse. They are simply to add meaning, purpose, and a caring community to your life. We all need a place where we can belong.

Is It Normal to Really Like Being Single Again?

Yes! I meet many singles right at the crisis point in their loss of a mate. They tell me they will never survive the loss. Many expect to simply die, but they don't. When I see them a few years later, they have made the difficult adjustment and are growing. A few more years after that, I have heard some say they really enjoy the new freedom that singleness has brought into their lives. They come and go as they please. They have many new friends. A sense of contentment has come into their lives. This does not necessarily mean they are committed to singleness forever. Some have said they would remarry if the right person for them came along, but the quest and the frantic searching that is sometimes a part of the singles world has ended for them. This is especially true of many singles whose children are grown and gone from home to their own pursuits. For many older singles, it is a delicate balance between freedom and loneliness.

What Do I Do If I Really Want to Remarry?

One lady told me she recently placed an ad in a singles newspaper. She thought if she described herself and the type of man she wanted to meet, the end result would be finding the right person. After numerous responses and dates, she declared the whole venture a disaster. Her reason for doing it was a form of desperation at not meeting any available men in her world.

The newspapers and magazines are filled with countless ways of meeting available singles. Many single-again people who really want to remarry may find themselves wondering whether or not they should enter some form of the match-a-mate game. To most people who have tried it, this seems a very stilted way to relate and more often than not, it produces unsatisfying results.

The first step in solving this dilemma is to decide whether or not you really want to remarry—and this is assuming that you are emotionally ready for it. If you are ready, you need to first realize it yourself. Self-affirmation is the first positive step. After you have made that decision, I think you have to be able to share it with your close and trusted friends. Some single-again people try to play the game of "Pretend you don't want to get married and someone will try to convince you that you should." A lot of good energy is lost at playing games. Being honest and up front with your feelings will help you and will also let others know where you are coming from. Right about here, you may be worrying about scaring off the prospects with your honesty. If you can frighten them away, let them run. Anyone who needs convincing is an unlikely candidate anyhow.

It is normal to want to remarry and to know that you are ready for it. It's okay to share that with others. Just don't print it on your new T-shirt!

Numerous women have asked me what I think about their asking a man over for dinner. I think it's great. A woman should have the freedom to take this kind of initiative once in a while. I know some men who are just waiting to be asked. They are just as afraid of doing the asking as women are. The obvious reason is fear of rejection.

While it is fine to let your intentions be known, don't be overbearing, don't come on too strong, and let relationships grow naturally. If they are to blossom, they will. If they appear to be dying, don't throw more fertilizer on them. Move on and be encouraged. Talking someone into an ongoing relationship can be hazardous to your health. Remember, as high as 60 percent of all second marriages fail.

Another wise thing to do if you want to remarry is to let God know about it and ask for His guidance and help in finding that right person for your life. I don't believe you should spend all your time sitting at home rocking and praying about it. I believe you should rock, pray, and then raise your antenna.

Taking a Close-up Look at a New Identity

Joining a new group, playing for a new team, moving to a new town, and starting a new job can all be a part of entering the world of sudden singleness. How you succeed in this area depends largely on how you feel about yourself. Your self-esteem is an axis upon which your new life will balance. There are three keys to taking a close look at your new identity.

1. *How do you see yourself?* Every morning you look into the mirror to see if you are still here, and you may be discouraged by your appearance—thinning hair, sagging stomach, multiplying wrinkles. Everything seems to be in a conspiracy to destroy your self-image. Oh, to be twenty-five and Mr. or Miss America!

You may take one of two approaches to what the mirror shows you. You can say, "All right," or you can say, "All wrong." A third alternative would be to break the mirror.

If you don't accept what you see in the mirror, you will project those feelings of self-doubt all day long. Your thoughts will be consumed by what you wish you looked like. You may even spend hundreds of dollars and hours of time in a personal rehabilitation project to improve your self-image.

On the other hand, if you are comfortable with what you see in the mirror, you will convey that also to those around you.

So how do you help yourself? Do you just keep on wishing? No, you begin to accept yourself. Accepting yourself does not mean that you are stuck in this area. You can make any physical changes if you so desire. But your basic acceptance is being able to say, "Thank You, God, for the gift of me. I accept the gift and thank You for it."

I meet singles in my travels who wish they were married. I meet some marrieds who wish they were single. I meet poor people who wish they were rich and rich people who wish they were richer. A great deal of time can be spent wishing you were different. Wanting to change the physical is just one side of self-image.

I sometimes ask people in counseling how they feel about themselves. Right away they point out specific reasons that they don't feel good about themselves. Physical appearance is often a leading cause (too fat, too thin). Lack of material possessions (money) is a close second, followed by personal problems (shyness, no friends). Too often they concentrate on what is wrong with them rather than on what they can change and improve. Some days I feel that 90 percent of the singles I meet suffer from a bad self-image. You are God's unique, unrepeatable miracle. God doesn't deal in junk. You are very special, no matter how you think you look in your mirror.

2. *How do others see you?* That's a tricky one. Even if you have a fair and rapidly improving self-image, you always wonder if others will like what they see. In order to enhance this, many people spend all their time trying to be people pleasers. Some even try to buy approval. I went to school with a very obnoxious boy who did not appeal to his classmates. Knowing this, he tried to buy their acceptance by inviting them to be his guests every day after school at the local snack shop. He tried desperately to buy friendship. The sad thing was that his schoolmates enjoyed his treats but rejected his friendship when he wasn't buying. It was a tragic experience for the boy, but it happens all the time. You cannot buy acceptance.

One way to help others see us better is to concentrate on being ourselves. "Candid Camera," the old television show, used the slogan "people caught in the act of being themselves." There is a freedom in being yourself. Maybe the biggest discovery any of us can make is to really know who we are, to be that person, and live that out.

The church where I currently work is in Hollywood, California. It is often referred to as the land of plastic impressions and relationships. Many who live there are caught up in the act of selling their image to others, and they end up not knowing who they really are. Sometimes we wonder if what we see is really what we are getting in another person.

Sometimes others view us through our honesty. Honesty is simply telling the truth. Because truth becomes so clouded in our world, we have a difficult time separating truth from fiction. A good relationship with another person always starts by our telling the truth about ourselves. When we carry that into every area of our lives, others will see us as trustworthy. Honesty involves being truthful with God, being honest with others, and being honest with ourselves. All three are tall orders to live up to.

There is a third way that others view us. They see us as affirmers. Unfortunately, the eighties seem to be an age of the lost art of affirmation.

A child comes home from school with a mammoth hunk of butcher paper covered with finger painting. As it's presented to you for your approval, you say kind and affirming things about both the artwork and the artist. You stick it on your refrigerator door and smile. You don't toss it in the garbage and inform the child that it's terrible. You affirm the work and the worker.

Adults need affirmation as much as children do. They want to hear someone say out loud, "You did well," or as they say down South, "You done good."

Encouragement to do greater things comes from the affirmation we receive in doing little things. We all need recognition. Do others see you as an affirmer?

3. *How does God see you?* Many divorced people would say that God only sees them as sinners, since divorce is a sin. They feel a hopelessness that affects other areas of their lives and can produce a bad self-image. They forget that God is in the forgiveness business. He is also in the loving business.

John 3:16 tells us that God loved the world. We are in that world and we are a very vital part of it. We are the recipients of His love. God sees us as a work of His creation. He sees us as His children and as a part of His family. He sees us as forgiven.

Sometimes you run into people who want to tell you how *they* think God sees *you.* When you meet them, take a quick walk in the opposite direction. Their business is often that of judging rather than caring. When you know how God sees you and can verify it from the Scriptures, you will not need their interpretations or judgments. As your new identity slowly comes into focus, you should be able to shout, "I am single, I am special, I am loved by God!"

Getting My New Identity Into Gear

There is a segment of Scripture found in Philippians 4:10–13, 19 that must have been written with a few singles in mind. In it, Paul sets forth three things that have helped him in his own growth and identity building.

The first one is learning to accept where you are. In verse 11 he says, "Not that I complain of want; for I have learned, in whatever state I am, to be content."

For Paul, this positive statement was framed by what he had gone through in his past: numerous shipwrecks, angry mobs, trials and imprisonments, questions about his leadership to his own people. Paul knew what he was talking about. He was seldom out of a crisis. Somehow, God gave him a spirit of confidence to know that where he was at any given moment in his life was all right—not always comfortable, but right.

In order to deal more effectively with your singleness, you have to accept it for now. Peace comes with acceptance and the knowledge that God is with you in your situation. You are not alone. There will be many days when you will want to look toward heaven and shout, "Why me, Lord?" If you listen, you might hear an answer coming back: *Why not you? I will give you the strength you need.*

The second thing Paul seems to be saying is to grow where you are. We have all heard the little slogan "Bloom where you are planted." It is sometimes difficult to believe that and do it when you would rather take your garden, your flowers, and your tools and move to an easier place to bloom.

Paul showed his own strength by doing some of his blooming while in prison. He longed to be free, but he used the experience to win some of his captors to a faith in Christ. His secret is in verse 13: "I can do all things in him who strengthens me." Paul wasn't growing on his own. Neither can you. God was infusing him daily with the strength he needed. That same growth-producing strength is available to you.

Some single-again people put off their growing until they feel better or their circumstances change. All that does is cause you to stagnate and watch things worsen. Still others wait to be rescued. Their hope is that they won't have to work too hard if someone else will do their growing for them. The real truth is that you have to do your own growing. No one can do it for you.

The third thing Paul talks about is building. In verse 19, he says, "And my God will supply every need of yours according to his riches in glory in Christ Jesus." You can't build anything until God supplies you with the materials. His building design for our lives is in the area of supplying the things we need rather than the things we want.

Many single-again people tell me they can't move ahead with their lives because they don't have everything, personally and materially, they had before singleness interrupted their journey. The problem is that they see what they *don't* have rather than what God *does* have.

Matthew 6:31 tells us, "Therefore do not be anxious, saying, 'What shall we eat?' or 'What shall we drink?' or 'What shall we wear?' " The writer goes on to say, "But seek first his kingdom . . . and all these things shall be yours as well" (verse 33).

Those are promises regarding God's supplying our construction materials. Accepting who you are, growing, and building are an important part of the process of creating a new identity as a single-now person. They help set you free from the growing threat of loneliness that engulfs so many newly single people.

Personal-Growth Questions

(For best results, work with a small group
or one other person.)

1. When you tell people that you are single, how do they usually respond?
2. What feelings do you have if their response is a negative one?
3. What is the most difficult thing you face in being single again?
4. Name one or two things you like most about being single.
5. Describe one or two things you are doing to try and get your singleness into gear.

3

I'm So Lonely I Could Die

Last year, 286,987 people died of loneliness! A shocking statistic. "I never heard that before," you say. You probably didn't for two reasons. First, no one keeps that kind of count. Second, few people, if any, die of loneliness—at least in a physical sense. However, I suspect that hundreds of thousands of people die a little emotionally each year as a result of loneliness.

In a recent seminar with over 250 singles, I asked the participants to write a one-word description of their greatest fear. As I tallied the cards while flying home after the seminar, I was shocked to find the vast majority had written the word *loneliness.*

Loneliness is not felt exclusively by those who have lost a "special someone" through death or divorce. It is an experience that everyone goes through at one time or another. Somehow the acute sting of it is more of a reality to those who have become suddenly single again.

During a recent counseling session, a young man confessed to me that he hated bars and drinking but that he spent most of his weekends there so he would not have to face his empty apartment and the loss of his wife. Perhaps you identify with him, as you have tried to fill empty moments with instant relationships. Some singles have told me they spend a great deal of time wandering through shopping malls just looking for people to talk with. Many of the lonely wanderers are looking for a few moments of happiness.

The world of psychology tells us there are three things that relieve loneliness and bring happiness to most people. They are: *something to do, someone to love,* and *something to look forward to.* Many of you reading this would probably want to draw a line through all three and say that the loss of your spouse has robbed you forever of all of them.

The reality of sudden singleness is that you will feel lonely. It's normal. It is also true that you will attempt to relieve that loneliness in a lot of crazy ways. One lady filled her apartment with singing birds. She had lots of noise and lots of cleaning up, but she soon found that you cannot instantly replace a spouse with six canaries. One of the real truths about dealing with loneliness is that you cannot replace a person with things or with another person. Our assignment in life is not to be substitutes for other people.

Loneliness has to be experienced for what it is. Loss and grief have to be sensed and felt as a part of the growth process. You cannot escape it by oversocializing or by going into seclusion and feeling sorry for yourself.

Sometimes we seek to fill the lonely silence with sound. It's not unlike the teenager who comes roaring home from school, flies to his bedroom, and turns on the stereo full blast. After about thirty seconds of airwave shock, his parent asks for it to be turned down or off. Most teenagers will say that they don't like quiet and being in their room alone. The sound of rock is, to them, the sound of people filling up the empty room.

We do the same thing. The first switch to go on in our car after the ignition switch is the radio. We seldom drive anywhere in quiet. The sounds of silence just remind us of the absence of people. Often, sounds are small life preservers that help us stay afloat on the sea of life and its attending loneliness.

There are many lonely people depicted in the Scriptures. Some of the leaders in Old Testament times found themselves lonely in their serving capacity. Some who tried to run from God's directions became the victims of loneliness. Elijah the prophet, after some of his greatest victories for God, found himself alone under a bush plagued by the desire to die. He was lonely and fearful, and it was not until God came to him that his loneliness began to pass.

Moses experienced the isolation and loneliness of leading a nation around in the wilderness. Jesus experienced the loneliness of going to the cross alone. The lines from a Negro spiritual express much of His life. The song says, "Jesus walked this lonesome valley, He had to walk it by Himself, Oh, nobody else could walk it for Him, He had to walk it by Himself."

Some of your journey through singles territory will be very lonely. I don't think there is a lonelier experience than going for the first time to a singles meeting. By just placing your body in the room, you are saying, "I'm single." The fear of rejection by those already there can be pretty strong.

It is easy to feel that you are just one more lonely person in a room full of lonely people.

Here are several realities regarding loneliness:

1. I will experience loneliness as a newly single person.
2. It is normal to feel lonely.
3. I will not die of loneliness.
4. Substitutions will not dissolve my loneliness.
5. I will grow through the experience.

My experience in counseling in this area has shown me that there are two distinct kinds of loneliness a newly single person faces. *The first relates to the person he is no longer with due to death or divorce.* Feelings go from wishing it were not so to the feelings of anger that it *is* so. In between both of these feelings is a great deal of fantasizing and an attempt at memory filing. Given some time and the honesty of facing and working through your feelings, healing begins to take place.

The second kind of loneliness deals with wanting another person, almost any other person, in your life—someone who will be there for you and bring meaning to your existence; a person to whom you would be significant. One of the greatest struggles in sudden singleness is in dealing with this kind of loneliness. Some respond to it by an endless chain of sexual relationships. Others go from singles meeting to singles meeting looking for someone, sometimes *anyone,* who will fill their void of loneliness. The kind of casual relationships that this invites is never satisfying for very long.

Negative Responses to Loneliness

There are as many responses to loneliness as there are people. I want to share some of the negative reactions I have seen in single people who are lonely.

1. *Run away and hide.* If you do this, you won't have to face the problem. Or even better, people will feel sorry for you and do for you what you need to be doing for yourself. Jonah in the Bible is a good example of someone who ran away and hid so that he would not have to face the people of Nineveh. Running away is becoming an increasing problem in our society. Our very mobility encourages it. It is difficult to hit a moving target.

Are you running from your loneliness? Can you run far enough?

2. *Pop a pill.* Got a headache? Take an aspirin. Got a heartache? Take a valium. Drug dependency is a common way of resolving almost any mental, psychological, emotional, or physical problem. As we run from the realities, the pile of pills grows higher. Uppers, downers, lifters, levelers!

Are you hooked on pills as a way to handle your loneliness?

3. *Eat six hot-fudge sundaes and a giant pizza.* Probably all of us, at one time or another, have raided the refrigerator in a moment of depression, anxiety, or loneliness. Did we feel better afterward? Generally not. The truth is you can't eat your problems away, even if your salivary glands seem to be telling you that you can. Overeating by lonely, socially outcast young people has been a recognized problem for years.

A new generation of singles may be not far behind. Are you trying to eat your way through your loneliness? What will you look like when you do, and how will your self-image be?

4. *Feel sorry for yourself.* Feeling sorry for yourself leads you into a place sometimes called Pity City. Once you have taken up residence there, your next move can be into the Valley of Depression. Hundreds of books are in print dealing with depression and how to cure it. Perhaps the best way is to prevent it by watching for the road signs that lead to it.

Self-pity usually starts by telling yourself that what happened to you is unfair. The implication is that it should have happened to someone else. You certainly did not deserve it. After you tell that to yourself long enough, you start telling it to others. All they have to do is confirm it, tell you they agree with you, and you are on the freeway to Pity City. Depression, an ultimate destination of many, becomes a cocoon in which to hide from life. It's a final prison of self-commiseration.

How much time a week do you spend feeling sorry for yourself?

5. *Become a social butterfly.* I meet many singles who try to replace their loneliness with an enormous amount of activities. There is nothing wrong with staying busy if you are not hiding behind it. It is only when activities keep you from facing your own struggles and realities that they take on a negative dimension. I asked one suddenly single-again cyclone if she ever slowed down or stopped long enough to catch her breath. Her response was, "If I do, I'm afraid of what I will find out." Coming, going, and doing in express fashion will more quickly result in fatigue than in a cure for loneliness.

6. *Go on a buying spree.* Women are often accused of buying a new dress or hat in order to make them feel better. All of us have had the experience of buying something we did not need or really want in order to ease the hurt or frustration of a situation. To be sure, it's a momentary high. The problem is that it doesn't last, and the original problem still remains. Will a bigger house, a sportier car, a new wardrobe, a younger man or woman, a month in Europe, really solve your loneliness problem? Are they answers or just minimal temporary relief?

Some Positive Responses to Loneliness

This is not a "do it and you will be fine" list. The following are merely some suggestions that other singles have found successful. You have to work at them or they will not be effective.

1. *Find a place to belong.* Most healthy relationships are built within the walls of a supportive community. Moving from the married world via death or divorce usually sends you in search of a new support structure. Many people feel they no longer belong to either world. Their support is gone and they feel very alone. There is a place for you to belong in the world of singleness. There are singles groups, singles clubs, singles tours, singles seminars and conferences, singles apartment complexes. There is no shortage of places and things. Some may be good for you and others may not.

A reality is that you do need a special place to belong. It may take some looking, adventuring, and time. You will know you have found your place because some of your loneliness will subside as you move into it.

2. Give your self-esteem a shot in the arm. Many of the single people I meet around the country have very low self-esteem. Some have experienced rejection to the point they believe they are not worth anything. Don't fall into this way of thinking. No matter what you have gone through, you are still God's unique, unrepeatable miracle.

In the Scriptures, Peter's self-esteem was at a very low point after his denial of Christ. It took an upper-room experience and a preaching experience later on to renew Peter's belief in himself as well as his belief in God.

A friend of mine has a favorite saying. When I leave him he always says, "Stay well and be good to yourself." Most of us don't have any problem with the staying-well part. A daily dose of vitamins and a good exercise routine will take care of that. The second part is a little more difficult. Being good to ourselves is recognizing that we are worth something, that we have gifts and deserve happiness.

The Scriptures speak about loving your neighbor as yourself. You *must* love yourself. At its finest point, that is what self-esteem is all about. Succeeding at a new challenge and making changes in your life all contribute to your self-esteem. What have you done for yourself lately that has made you feel good?

3. Get into the physical. The lady in a jogging suit and running shoes dropped into a front-row chair in my seminar. I asked her if she ran. Her breathless response was, "Ran all the way over here this morning. Several miles. Plan to run home when we are finished. Never ran until my divorce. Needed to get out of the pits. Been running ever since."

Obviously, running isn't an answer to loneliness for everyone, but it does have advantages. Getting into physical activities gets the body moving. It demands something from you when you don't feel like giving it. Your mind and your body are interconnected. It's difficult to feel lonely and sorry for yourself after you have just run two or three miles. Sports can also be enjoyed with others. Get into something and take some lessons, if needed. Get yourself moving.

4. *Set some goals.* The motto on the little wall hanging said, "Shoot at nothing and that's exactly what you will hit." Many newly single people have no goals. If they do have any, they are of the contingency variety. They are based upon someone else's reaction, response, or plans. Having a goal and working toward it gives purpose and meaning to life. Writing this book did not happen until I set the goals and then began to implement them a day at a time.

The Scriptures are full of accounts of goal-oriented people. God the Architect drew up the plans, and His followers had the opportunity to carry them out.

I have always dreamed of running in a marathon. I only dream about the start and the finish. It is hard to dream about the agony of what lies between. I know that in order for me to reach that goal, though, I have to set apart time to train. Training means running from fifty to sixty miles a week. That's the catch. I don't want to take the time to run that far each week. So I run a couple of miles a day and go on dreaming.

If you are going to set some goals, set some attainable ones first. Set the big ones later on. Always celebrate when you reach one of your goals. You deserve the party!

5. *Get some help.* If your loneliness seems to become your prison and you feel you are unable to escape, don't hesitate to get some professional counseling help. Sometimes the roots of loneliness are tied to other things in our lives, and only therapy can bring some resolution to the struggle. Don't be afraid to look for answers in the skills of others. And remember, counseling takes time. There are no instant answers to problems that may have accrued over a period of years.

6. *Talk to God about it.* God is aware of all the problems a person can have. Back in the Garden of Eden, God recognized one of Adam's original needs. He said, "It is not good that the man should be alone; I will make him an help meet for him" (Genesis 2:18 KJV). Some of you will read this and say, "I wish it were that easy. Do I just ask God and—*zap!*"

No, but God is aware of our loneliness when we experience it. It is and always has been a part of the human condition. God can move in different ways in our lives when we invite Him to fill some of the lonely voids.

His first promise to us was set in cement. The writer of Hebrews put it this way: "I will in no wise fail thee, Neither will I in any wise forsake thee" (Hebrews 13:5 PHILLIPS).

In your loneliness and in mine, God is right there, backing us up with His promises. He isn't moving out on us, divorcing us, or dying on us. *He is there!* I know He doesn't always do things on our timetable. Our schedule usually says RIGHT NOW. God seems to say, *When I am ready, then* you *will be ready.*

Sharing your needs, your struggles, and your loneliness with God in prayer is a positive step. Inviting God to help meet those needs in His own way is another step. Here is a short prayer that you can say:

> God, I'm so lonely. I know that's human. I invite You to come with Your strength, power, and love into the very center of my loneliness. Sweep away the cobwebs that tie me up, and help me to start climbing the ladder of growth. Amen.

Loneliness is the feeling that you are alone on the journey through life, and no one cares about your joys and sorrows. Perhaps someone once did, but he or she is no longer around.

Working through your loneliness is a time of rebuilding. It's a time for evaluation and sorting things out. It is also a time for looking deep inside yourself. It's a special time for reflection, meditation, and future planning. It's turning a negative experience into a positive, growth-producing one. It's developing a plan that won't leave you stuck at the crossroads of loneliness and self-pity.

Loneliness can be a rare gift that keeps us in touch with our humanity. It moves us toward a deeper relationship with God and our neighbor.

Loneliness will always be a part of the journey for the suddenly single-again person. Instead of a liability, it can be a great gift from God that helps you grow.

Personal-Growth Questions

(For best results, work with a small group
or one other person.)

1. What is the loneliest thing for you about being single again?
2. At what time during the week do you feel most lonely?
3. When loneliness seems to trap you and push you toward depression, what do you usually do to resolve it?
4. Of the negative responses to loneliness listed in this chapter, what one or ones do you most identify with?
5. Of the positive responses to loneliness, which one helps you the most?

4

I Need All the Friends I Can Get

In the last chapter, I shared some positive ways to handle the struggle with loneliness. One of those ways was to find a place to belong—in other words, a supportive and sustaining community.

In a book titled *Loneliness: The Experience of Emotional and Social Isolation,* Robert Weiss explores the many problems of loneliness. In the last pages of the book, he offers a solution to this haunting problem. He says:

> I can offer no method for ending loneliness other than the formation of new relationships that might repair the deficit responsible for the loneliness. And I think this solution ordinarily is not easy. If it were, there would be fewer lonely people.

Writing in the April 1981 issue of *Psychology Today* magazine, Daniel Yankelovich says:

> The hunger for deeper personal relationships shows up in our research findings as a growing conviction that a me-first, satisfy-all-my-desires attitude leads to relationships

that are superficial, transitory, and ultimately unsatisfying. Our survey shows that 70% of Americans now recognize that while they have many acquaintances, they have few close friends, and they experience that as a serious void in their lives. Moreover, two out of five, 41%, state they have fewer close friends than they had in the recent past.

Charlie Brown, in the "Peanuts" comic strip, makes a statement every so often that he needs all the friends he can get. As you look at the endless stream of characters drifting through Charlie's life, you quickly understand what he means. He needs friends who won't pull the football away when he is about to kick it, and friendly trees that won't ensnare his kite when he flies it.

You and I are not unlike good old Charlie Brown. We need friends—good ones we can trust—understanding and caring ones who will be there in any and every circumstance and situation.

In the world of the suddenly single-again person, that "best friend," in the form of one's spouse, is no longer there. Sometimes even the friends you made through your spouse disappear. You may find yourself, for the first time, very alone. At first, reaching out to others can feel very uncomfortable. It is a time for relational rebuilding, and that is a slow process.

The Different Levels of Relationships

Relationships are built on many different levels. Most of us are inhibited just enough to want others to do all the reaching out toward us. That's usually safe, for it puts us in charge of the response we choose to make. When we reach out to others first, we run the risk of their rejection, and that puts them in charge. Here are several types of relationships we all encounter.

1. *Random relationships.* There are a great number of come-and-go relationships drifting through most of our lives. There is the clerk at the supermarket who bags our groceries and exchanges small talk. There is the service-station mechanic we see every three months for car maintenance. The list also includes the mailman, the paperboy, the friends at our church, and our children's friends' parents. You could add a whole lot more to your own list.

These are the surface people in our lives. Our conversations usually consist of "Hi, how are you?" "Fine, how are you?" These people serve our own needs at an operational level. We don't want to know how they are. We don't have time to find out. Even worse, we really don't care, because we have no real involvement with them. They are merely our "maintenance people." We know their names and faces, but not their lives and struggles. We choose no deeper involvement than we have.

2. *Social relationships.* There are people in our lives whom we socialize with. We bowl, party, picnic, vacation, and camp with them. We invest ourselves recreationally with this group, but we rarely relate on a deep emotional level.

Many of you single-again people have had the experience of going to a social event attended by couples who were once a part of your world. It doesn't take long for you to feel very out of place. The visible togetherness of others just accentuates your aloneness. That special someone is no longer with you. Some singles have shared with me how they have run teary eyed from these kinds of events.

3. *Deep relationships.* Sometimes in my seminars, I ask the question "How many of you have a deep, intimate relationship with someone other than your spouse; a relationship of over ten years' endurance?" Usually not many hands are raised, but most people express the honest desire for this in their lives.

In the Bible, David and Jonathan had a deep friendship. It did not come about overnight. It took time to grow into an enduring relationship.

Few of us have the time to invest in more than one or two deep relationships. Our busy schedules push us toward an "instant intimacy" with other people. Our cry is, "Bare your soul. Tell me your history, and let's have a deep relationship." The problem with this is that friendships of lasting and enduring quality do not happen this way. Our world is in a hurry, but you can't rush the growth of a significant relationship. Perhaps the line from Paul Simon's "59th Street Bridge Song" needs to be re-heard: "Slow down, you move too fast. Got to make the morning last."

Deep relationships involve listening, sharing, caring, and a great deal of personal commitment. A relationship with depth is always an investment.

We could call these three levels of relationship building "stepping-stones." All relationships begin on a random or casual level. We decide whether or not we will elevate them from there to the social level. Once at the social level, we decide whether we will move toward intimacy or depth with that person. All the while, we look for a commonality that draws us to another person. There is a certain chemistry in all relationships. Both people have to invest equal energy in the relationship. One person alone cannot make it happen. Sometimes our most meaningful relationships begin in strange ways. You can't plan them any more than you can set aside a day to go shopping for a new spouse. Relationships begin when we are available to them. That essentially means they will not happen if you are hiding in your closet or stuck in your rocker looking out the window at life passing by.

I meet some people who try to spiritualize their lack of good relationships by stating that God will send friends to them when He is ready. I deeply believe in God's direction in our lives. I also believe that we have to take the initiative and push ourselves out into the mainstream of life. Fishing in the bathtub can be a frustrating experience.

Let me clarify here that in talking about relationship building in this chapter we are not talking about finding a husband or wife. We are talking about finding friends of both sexes. It is possible, though, that a relationship can bloom into a marriage. That would be a serendipity.

Building relationships means bringing meaningful people into your life at many different levels. Many single-again people have only one objective in mind: Find a person to marry as soon as possible. The pressure and panic that results from this kind of pursuit is enormous. An alternate response to the marriage-partner search is to see how many relationships you can sustain while "playing the field." The "one-night stand" is sometimes synonymous with this kind of behavior. People are used and discarded for self-gratification rather than relationship building.

When two people marry, they already have a relationship with each other. In-laws and relatives on both sides of the family form an instant circle of additional accepted relationships. Divorce and death can strip away this close circle and leave a person standing alone. Looking into the world of singleness means restructuring and building new and meaningful relationships.

Jesus' Circles of Relationships

A model in relationship building is Jesus. We will gain more from looking at how He built and needed relationships than "how He survived as a single." Relationships were important to Him, and He gave quality time to them. The closest and most intimate relationship Jesus had on earth appears to have been with John, the beloved disciple. Beyond His immediate family, John was a relationship priority with Jesus. We are not sure about the "why" in this relationship, but the Scriptures portray the deep love and intimacy between Jesus and John. It was a special friendship.

On another level, Peter, James, and John seemed to form the inner circle that Jesus counted close to Himself. He confided in them. He asked special support from them. They were near Him in His moments of triumph and agony. They were as different from each other as night from day. Yet their friendship with Jesus was deep.

On other levels of relationships with Jesus, we have the 12 disciples; after that, the 70, the 120, and the 500. Beyond all of these were the crowds that followed Jesus everywhere.

They reached out to touch Him, and He touched them back. They went their way, and He went His.

As you explore the Scriptures, you can quickly see where Jesus spent most of His time. The disciples were His inner circle. They shared in His life. Jesus knew that He could not give quality time to everyone.

At yet another place in Jesus' friendship circle stood Mary, Martha, and Lazarus. Scripture indicates that it was to their home Jesus went for refuge, renewal, and rest. All of us need a center like that to retreat to—away from the demands of life—distant from the reaching hands of others and their constant expectancies. We need a place and a circle of friends in which to let down our guard and be ourselves in a relaxed way. This is a very important part of relationship building. Where is your special place to rest and be renewed while the world races by?

The Value of Deep Relationships

If the comment by researcher Yankelovich at the beginning of this chapter is true, perhaps we should take a look at the value of those relationships we need and what they will add to our lives.

1. *Acceptance.* We all have that basic human need to be accepted by others as we are—warts and all. We generally only reveal little bits and pieces of ourselves as we get to know others. We are really testing them to see if there is a point of nonacceptance where they will cut us off and the relationship will go no further. Sometimes this is done very adeptly in the dating process. Hours are spent in prepping

for a date so that someone will see us as we would like them to see us. Only as our acceptance level with the other person climbs do we lower our preparation time. After marriage, we seldom give much thought to how we look to the other person.

As children, we are told to make a good impression on people. We will be liked and accepted if we do. One day my doorbell rang, and I raced through the house from my backyard gardening to answer it. As the sweat and dirt ran down my face, I opened the door, only to stand nose to nose with one of the most immaculately dressed women I had ever known. She was in my singles group and was dropping off some fliers.

Standing there in my cutoffs, shirtless and dripping, I certainly did not look like anything close to a senior staff minister at a large church. Her comment was, *"Jim,"* with what seemed to have a large question mark behind it. I found myself racing through an apology for the way I looked, explaining that I was knee-deep in gardening. I was desperately concerned about her continued acceptance of me as her pastor, even though I did not appear pastorly looking.

From time to time, we all get caught when we are not looking the way we would like to look. Life seems to be one long prep course in acceptance.

2. *Trust.* A deep relationship with another person has trust as one of its root ingredients. Without trust, there can be no depth in a relationship.

I speak with many people in divorce counseling who have had their trust violated. Perhaps their husbands or wives ran off with another person after an affair was discovered. They wonder if they will ever be able to trust another person again.

Trust is an earned commodity as a relationship or friendship grows. When a friend says he will pick you up at eight, you place trust in his promise. If it is constantly violated and he is habitually late, the trust level goes down. Building trust is believing promises as you see them lived out.

God has placed an infinite amount of trust in you and me as His creative work. We return that trust by believing His Word and accepting the promises it contains. Our trust level in God grows as we watch those promises being fulfilled in our lives. When He says He is with us—*He is really with us!* A deep relationship with a friend says, "I literally trust you with my life." A deep relationship with God says the same thing.

3. *Lack of jealousy.* Can you have a deep and meaningful relationship with someone of whom you are very jealous? I don't believe you can. Jealousy becomes a noose around a relationship that strangles the life from it. Jealousy ran rampant in the Early Church in the Bible. Paul constantly spoke about it in his letters. Even the disciples had to deal with it as they struggled for the highest position in the kingdom they thought Jesus was setting up on earth.

Jealousy is a part of our human situation, but it destroys relationships. Celebration replaces jealousy. Instead of being jealous of my friends' gifts, talents, promotions, success, and wealth, I can choose to celebrate them. If I want the best for them, I will realize that I am not in competition with them. I am in friendship with them.

4. Honesty. When faced with a conflict or a decision, it's so easy to go from friend to friend collecting opinions. We call this a "pooling of ignorance." What we are doing most of the time is listening for only what we want to hear. Too few of us tell the truth to others. We are afraid that if we do, our relationships with them will falter and end. It is always interesting to me that the scriptural directive is to "speak the truth in love" (Ephesians 4:15 PHILLIPS). Truth, when spoken, demands a gentle handling. It is not something that we throw at people and hope they will catch. It is fragile and demands a loving touch. Only those who are our real friends and love us most will tell us the truth. Honesty will always hurt a lot less when it comes from someone who loves us and whom we love in return.

5. Loyalty. Loyalty in relationships says, "I will stand with you no matter what. If you do something I disagree with, I will tell you, but I will still be loyal to you with my friendship." Some of the best visual expressions of loyalty seem to come from animals. The world could certainly use a few more Lassies, Silvers, or Old Paints. Loyalty is the cement of friendship. The one thing Jesus' disciples had a difficult time with was loyalty. They enjoyed recognition when the miracles were happening, but when the clouds of the Crucifixion hung over them, they wanted to hide.

6. Being there. Single-again people have often shared with me that the toughest part of their day is coming home from work when they know that no one will be there to greet them. Loneliness is intensified at that point.

God has created us with a burning need to have people around us who are significant to us and care for us. This doesn't mean you need a party every day when you come home from work so that the house won't be empty. It does mean that you need to have special people in your life who will be there for you when you need them.

Hospital calling has always been uncomfortable for me. I feel pretty helpless and realize I can do little to enhance a person's healing process. I pray, encourage, make small talk, smile, and leave. Later people thank me for the visit. I wonder why. Then they say something like, "Thanks for just being there." Building relationships helps us learn that there are people who will be there for us when we need them.

7. *Spiritual resources.* Have you ever had a time in your life when a crisis hit you full force? I have. The shock and hurt were so great that it seemed my faith in God and His promises had gone on vacation.

It's a time like this that a trusted friend can offer his or her spiritual resources and strength to you. I recently called a friend in the midst of one of my chaos times. It was reassuring to know that someone on the other end of the phone, over two thousand miles away, listened intently as I shared my struggle. The simple words, "We will have faith for you," were what I really needed to hear. I am not always strong enough to have the faith I need in troubled times. I need my friends and their spiritual aid.

The years of developing deep relationships with people take on more meaning as we get older. There is a richness in friendships that gives our lives meaning and continuity. Our spiritual growth is not a solo flight. It is a shared journey.

One of the ongoing struggles in the world of singleness centers around the intensity of relationships. The priority of many singles is finding the ultimate person for them—a potential mate. There is nothing wrong with this unless it becomes a pursuit that denies the building of other healthy relationships.

I have suggested to many singles across the country that they would experience less pressure if they built more brother-sister relationships.

You are seated in the corner booth at McDonald's, after your midweek singles gathering, with a member of the opposite sex. A few people from your group drift by, greeting you as they pass. The next day you might receive several calls asking if you have something serious going on with the person you were with. You get a little upset and tell the callers that you just have a nice friendship with that person.

The truth is that single people need a few friends of the opposite sex who are simply *friends.* Many men and women have told me that they were not ready to even consider marriage or involved dating, but they did feel the need to spend time talking with someone other than members of their own sex.

It seems human nature in singles groups to want to match people up. Resist the urge. It won't help you, and it certainly won't help the other person.

Another way to take some of the pressure out of relating is to develop the brother-sister relationships I mentioned a moment ago. The friendships developed within the Christian community should take on the quality of a brother-sister relationship. The actions, conduct, and treatment of your Christian brothers and sisters should parallel that of your family.

Charlie Brown is right. I need all the friends I can get. So do you. Are you growing some good friendships?

Personal-Growth Questions

(For best results, work with a small group
or one other person.)

1. Write down the three most meaningful relationships you have in your life right now and what you feel each one contributes to you.
2. What kind of relationship do you feel most in need of right now?
3. Do you feel more comfortable giving or receiving in a relationship?
4. Where do you find your supportive community?
5. If you have a healthy brother-sister relationship with a member of the opposite sex, how do you feel this helps you in your life?

5

It's a Jungle Out There

It was time for questions at the end of a singles seminar. A hand at the back of the room went up very slowly. As I pointed in that direction, a quavering voice stammered out the question: "Would you s-s-s-s-ay something about s-s-s-s-ex?" I responded by saying that sex was fun. Several laughed while others remained silent. I knew that wasn't the answer the questioner had desired. My second response was to acknowledge that this is a genuine problem for many single-again people. The audience breathed easier and nodded their heads in agreement.

Of all the issues I have been asked about by singles over the last ten years, the question of how to handle singleness and sexuality is the most frequent.

There seems to be an assumption afloat on the sea of singleness that after a person has been married and enjoyed a sexual relationship, when they become single again they simply can't live without sex. After watching a few TV soaps, daytime or evening variety, it would appear that one of life's great pastimes is playing musical beds. Many of those people jumping in and out are either divorced, about to be divorced, having an affair, or single. If we absorb what we witness on television long enough, we might be convinced that everyone lives that way.

A lady approached me on a Sunday morning at the end of our singles class. She stated that she was newly divorced and wanted to know why, as the word got out in her community, many of her former spouse's male friends were calling her and asking her if she had any "needs" they could help fulfill. (I hesitate to tell you what they really asked.) It may have happened to you. Her question was, "Why?" I am not sure of the answer, but I have heard the question from many singles.

Sex and Sexuality

We could define sex or the sex act as a biological function. That is the level at which many people deal with it. On a higher level, we have to deal with sexuality as a total package. That package does not just consist of a biological function. It includes intimacy, love, feelings, consideration, kindness, caring, support, and trust. It involves one's whole emotional being. It is involvement with another person that is total and complete, and continues that way through life. This is not easy to come to grips with. Many people never get beyond shortsighted sex to understand the longer view and its involvements. Is your view and understanding of sexuality short-circuited by recognizing only the biological-need level?

Ours is a sex-saturated society. Much of today's advertising is tied to sexual identification. You are definitely out of step if you don't go with the stream of today's sexual thinking. Rather than just admitting it's a big problem and talking about something else, let's explore some of the reasons that lie behind the sexual issue.

1. Loneliness. A few pages back, I talked about this problem. Many singles have shared with me that they became sexually involved with another person just to eliminate their gripping loneliness for an evening. In the deep moments of the intimacy of a sexual relationship, their loneliness seemed to vanish. The problem is that it returns again after the experience ends. The supposed cure becomes, in effect, a Band-Aid for the problem.

We all know how good a hug feels when we are hurting. It makes us feel warm, cared for, accepted. A sexual encounter can bring about those same feelings, even temporarily. It can be a way of telling yourself that you are okay after all and that you won't be lonely anymore. But in the lines of a pop song, "There's got to be a morning after." On that morning dawns the realization that you have only traded some of your loneliness for short-lived affection.

2. Desire to be loved. There is probably no better feeling than the knowledge that we are loved in significant ways by others. I meet many people who are love starved. They often reach out in frantic efforts for any kind of love.

In a marriage, everyone experiences some form of love from their mates. That love gives a feeling of security. In the world of the suddenly single, often after a severe rejection, there is a deep desire to prove that one is lovable.

There are many ways to feel loved without sexual involvement. There is an old saying: "Never replace the future on the altar of the immediate." Many singles seem to be going the instant-intimacy route in an effort to prove that they can be loved right now. Love in the future is too far away to wait for.

3. *Manipulation and intimidation.* "If I don't go to bed with him, he won't ask me out again." I have heard that statement hundreds of times from the single women I meet. It sounds like the threat of the hijacker who says to the pilot of the plane, "Fly me to Cuba, or I will explode this bomb." It's called intimidation, and our society has become expert at its usage. We hear it on all sides. Unions ask for more money and threaten to strike if they don't get it. We threaten to sue our neighbor if his dog doesn't stay off our lawn. We are living in a litigation-happy society. The message, in all areas, is "Give me what I want or I will punish you physically, emotionally, socially, mentally, or financially."

When a sexual encounter is traded for an evening on the town because of the fear that there will be no more evenings on the town, someone is being manipulated. The tragedy is that this can become a way of life. Sexual bartering is about as prevalent as window-shopping.

The victims of this sexual intimidation-manipulation game come away feeling used and conned. Their self-esteem goes begging in the process of having their feelings ignored.

4. *Sexual rights.* I have heard numerous single-again people say that they have a right to a sexual relationship with any consenting adult they choose. As a professor in my college used to say, "Your rights extend to the end of your nose." A sexual encounter involves two people. Do the rights of the other person supersede yours, or do yours supersede his or hers?

Your rights and the rights of others are precious and guarded responsibilities. When someone else is used for your own gratification, his or her rights are being violated.

5. *Self-gratification.* Many sexual encounters are simply trips into self-gratification. The seventies have been described as the "me first" decade—looking out for yourself and stepping on others to fulfill your own needs. You hurt others so that you can be satisfied, and you try to catch the brass ring for yourself. How long can your needs be met at someone else's expense? Before long, the other person will feel hurt and used, and grow increasingly calloused toward you.

Most singles organizations have a problem with a group of wandering singles known as "body snatchers." They are the marauders who invade singles groups to satisfy their own sexual needs and experience another conquest.

I asked one woman how she handled an approach by a "body snatcher." She said, "I laugh a lot, look him in the eye and say, 'You've got to be kidding,' and walk away." This is probably the best reaction. And in case women readers are thinking that men are always the marauders, let me tell you that there are lots of women in the seducing business.

You may be thinking that this sounds like a description of a swinging-singles group you might read about in the newspaper. My experience has been that these problems exist in church-oriented singles groups everywhere. The only difference is that they are not talked about openly in the religiously oriented group.

6. *Everyone is doing it.* We live in an age of conscious collapse. We are easily seduced by the thought that "everyone is doing it," "everyone is buying it," "everyone is wearing it," and "everyone is going there." Clothing fads tell us to get into our signature jeans or we will be stared at when we go out. The insinuation is that we had better get with it or we will be out of step with the world.

This same mind set carries into the area of sexual involvement. Society says that everyone is having sex with everyone else and that you are quite abnormal if you don't participate. Group pressure to conform and not be left at the gate when the race starts begins to swallow you up.

You can't collect your standards from the crowd. They have to come from you, without external pressure. Absorbing others' views and standards leaves you never quite sure about yourself. No one enjoys living with uncertainties.

You are *you.* You are not everyone else!

7. *Can't live without sex.* I often listen to this myth as it is passed around singles groups. The logic seems to be that the sex drive and sexual fulfillment are human needs that must be met whether inside or outside of marriage.

I have met many singles who are celibate and have been that way for some years. They have made a choice for their single-now status. They are not strange-looking folks with little horns protruding from their ears. They are happy, growing people who have simply exercised their right to choose for themselves and are living that choice out until marriage changes it.

Several recent magazines have reported a growing interest in celibacy for singles. It could well be that we have reached our saturation point in the sexual jungle, and some people are looking for more meaningful ways to handle their sexuality. No one is saying that this is easy, but neither is running a marathon. The end result is the important part. Always remember that sex was made *for* man and woman, not man for sex.

Just talking about the reasons for conflict in the area of facing sex as a single-again person does not solve the problem. Many single-again people are looking for justification for what they want to do. Others are simply trying to decide what to do. As one man recently stated, "Don't tell me to take more cold showers. My water bill is high enough already."

Three Attitudes Toward Dealing With the Sexual Struggle

Attitude one. Sex is okay—anytime, anyplace, with anyone who is a consenting adult and of legal age. Does that sound a little like the last television show you watched? Probably! This attitude is held by a large segment of the singles world today. It follows the slogan "If it feels good, do it." We could probably call this sexual liberty or sexual freedom. We forget that freedom always comes with responsibilities attached. In the world of sexual license, there are seldom thoughts of responsibilities. This is, at best, random sex.

Attitude two. Sex is okay—anytime, anyplace, with anyone of legal age, but only if you have a "meaningful relationship" with the person. The question that arises here is, "What does meaningful mean?" It is a relative term. If I said I had a meaningful breakfast this morning, would you know what I had? It could be two vitamins and a glass of juice, or the whole breakfast special at my neighborhood restaurant. What is known as meaningful to one person may lack meaning to another person.

Meaningful in the above context could mean you have had three dates with the same person before you engage in sex. It could mean sixty dates. It could mean engagement.

Some people would call this selective sex. Many singles find themselves in this situation. They don't want to be known as bed hoppers, so they opt for a smattering of involvement to justify a sexual relationship.

Attitude three. Sex is a gift from God, and it comes with great responsibilities to the participants. It is best enjoyed to its fullest within the context of a marital relationship. Sounds rather restrictive, doesn't it? You might wonder if anyone in today's world really believes this. Contrary to what you might think, there are many single-again persons who believe that this attitude is the right one for them and seek to live by it.

These three attitudes are widely scattered throughout the singles community. Let me ask you several questions to help you sharpen your own focus:

1. Which one of the three attitudes describes where you are in your own thinking right now? Be honest.
2. How did you arrive at that attitude? What led you to it and what or who influenced you?
3. Is it the best and right place for you to be? Why?
4. Where do you think God wants you to be? Why?

What I have discovered from talking to thousands of single people about this subject is that many of them have never really thought much about where they stand. They have developed a conditional stand, a sort of "We'll see what happens and what kind of opportunities come up, then decide." Living by situation ethics is always precarious. You never have a solid foundation under you. You are totally subject to your emotions of the moment. It's a little like standing on a cloud.

I believe that people with well-thought-through convictions draw respect. People who live in the cracks of life are never taken too seriously.

The above questions will provide you with a lot of homework. If you do it, you will find your struggles in this area greatly reduced.

What Does God Think About Sex and Singleness?

That's a good question, and many people don't want to know. If you have decided to follow God, then you need to know and wrestle with the implications.

The Scriptures talk about a general principle for all our behavior in 1 Corinthians 10:31: "So, whether you eat or drink, or whatever you do, do all to the glory of God." The "whatever" is pretty comprehensive. It includes relating sexually in your life. Most people would not think that. They would look at the obvious things like fun, hobbies, conversation, and jobs. Paul put the *all* in there for our own safety in making decisions.

Some years ago, a friend suggested that I always consider two questions when I had to make a decision in my life. The first was, "Can this be done to the glory of God?" The second was, "Is this the best that God intends for me?" When those two questions are used in the sexual-involvement evaluation, you might come to some rapid solutions in dealing with the issue.

In a more specific way, Paul speaks again in 1 Corinthians 6:13–20. He starts by talking about food again. I guess he knew that would get our attention every time:

"Food is meant for the stomach and the stomach for food"—and God will destroy both one and the other. The body is not meant for immorality, but for the Lord, and the Lord for the body. And God raised the Lord and will also raise us up by his power. Do you not know that your bodies are members of Christ? Shall I therefore take the members of Christ and make them members of a prostitute? Never! Do you not know that he who joins himself to a prostitute becomes one body with her? For, as it is written, "The two shall become one flesh." But he who is united to the Lord becomes one spirit with him. Shun immorality. Every other sin which a man commits is outside the body; but the immoral man sins against his own body. Do you not know that your body is a temple of the Holy Spirit within you, which you have from God? You are not your own; you were bought with a price. So glorify God in your body.

These are some of the strongest words Paul spoke regarding the use of our bodies. The people in his day faced the same issues and struggles that we face today. The only difference between Paul's time and ours is that we get better media coverage.

The single-again Christian listens to the logic the world offers in the sexual area. He battles with his or her own emotions and feelings, but must still measure them against what the Scriptures teach. It is only then that answers begin to become clear.

A Christian's sexual ethics and conduct need to be determined by the understanding of what God really had in mind when He gave man and woman the gift of sex. This gift was certainly a great idea. It was given for enjoyment and pleasure as well as procreation. But it was also given in trust. That trust was that it would be used within the boundaries that God intended for it to be used. I believe the Scriptures are clear in stating that those boundaries are within the framework of the marriage relationship.

That does not mean that having a sexual relationship outside of marriage is not fun. It does mean that it will never bring you God's intended best in the way of enjoyment and fulfillment. Perhaps this is why so many sexually worn-out singles ask me if there is some other answer in this area that they missed along the way.

God knew what He was doing when He designed men and women. It's only when we try to do the redesigning that we get into trouble. Getting mad at God because you don't like His design, and doing your own thing will not bring you happiness.

Sex is a choice, and choices always bring responsibilities. As a single-again person, you won't be around too long before you are confronted with the sexual issue. Your own rationalizing may click into gear before you have a chance to check into God's best intentions. Your own needs, desires, feelings, frustrations, and lack of love and loving may dominate your thinking. Let me share several suggestions for you to think about as you work to resolve this issue.

1. Really check out for yourself what the Scriptures teach. Read the references and commentaries.
2. Read a few good books that deal expansively with sexuality, singleness, and marriage. (*See* the reading list at the end of the book.)
3. Talk to God about it. He made the promises to help you through your struggles. Tell Him how you feel and where you need help.
4. Learn to share your struggles and feelings in this area with other single Christians. Ask them what they do and what answers they have found for their lives. Don't push the topic under the rug in your singles group. Talk it through.
5. When you come to a place of deep conviction in your life, don't club other people with it. Try saying, "I have found this to be the best way for me to live." Leave others free to live as they choose. All you can do is share where you are and how you arrived there.

I said at the start of this chapter that this was a tough area. You won't resolve it in the next three minutes. Even after you do resolve it for yourself, you will still struggle with it a lot. Just rest assured you are not alone. *God cares!*

Personal-Growth Questions

(For best results, work with a small group
or one other person.)

1. What is the single biggest problem for you in dealing with your sexuality as a single-again person?
2. Of the three attitudes toward sex discussed in this chapter, which one describes you, and why?
3. Why do you feel the issue of sexuality and singleness is seldom discussed in church-related singles groups?
4. How free do you feel to tell someone you are on a date with about your sexual attitudes?
5. What problems are you struggling with right now in the sexual area, and what are you doing to resolve them?

6

Get Going, Get Growing

There are five major building blocks in the growth process for those who are suddenly single again. All of them deal with change, and all of them bring big adjustments into your new life. These building blocks are personal, social, vocational, sexual, and spiritual. In this chapter, we want to take a closer look at spiritual growth.

The crisis of the death or divorce of a mate can affect a person's spiritual growth in many ways. Some who are non-spiritually oriented prior to this crisis become spiritually connected during and as a result of it. Others who were connected can become separated, disjointed, and adrift from God and growth. Still others get mad at God and blame Him for letting their tragedy happen.

One of my goals in this book is to help you examine and evaluate your life and growth as a single-again person. A primary key to your growth is found in the spiritual area.

What Is Spiritual Growth?

In a recent conversation with a person in a singles group, the question was asked, "What is spiritual growth, and how do you really know if you are growing spiritually?" Let's try to answer that from a scriptural and practical point of view.

The Bible speaks a lot about growing. Writing to the Early Church at Ephesus, Paul says, "Rather, speaking the truth in love, we are to grow up in every way into him who is the head, into Christ" (Ephesians 4:15). Peter tells us to "grow in the grace and knowledge of our Lord and Savior Jesus Christ" (2 Peter 3:18). In his first letter, Peter states, "So put away all malice and all guile and insincerity and envy and all slander. Like newborn babes, long for the pure spiritual milk, that by it you may grow up to salvation" (1 Peter 2:1, 2). Jesus, in His earthly ministry, talked repeatedly of growth and used many agrarian examples to illustrate His points. He spoke of planting seeds, growing wheat, and harvesting crops.

A crisis can be a definite deterrent to our growth, or it can cause us to grow more than ever. I think we decide within ourselves which it will be. In his letter to the Romans, Paul says, "And we know that all things work together for good to them that love God, to them who are the called according to his purpose" (Romans 8:28 KJV). This verse does not say that everything that happens to us is good. It says that God will take everything and work it together so that the end result is good.

Losing a mate is usually not regarded as good. But out of this, God can bring good and cause tremendous growth in your life. Let's look at the ways this can happen.

Spiritual growth is believing God's promises. We build a trust level with God the same way we build a trust level with other human beings. Trust grows when it is put to the test.

Our muscles develop only when they are tested, not when they lie dormant. I am always amazed when people tell me they have prayed for something and are shocked when God answers them. That's strange. He promised He would answer if we asked. We sometimes have to learn renewed trust in God by trusting Him with the little things in our lives, before we can trust Him with the bigger things. His promises are to be claimed, not just memorized.

Spiritual growth is removing fears from your life. In another chapter, I will talk more about fear. Let me just share one of God's promises about fear now. In 2 Timothy 1:7, the writer says, "For God hath not given us the spirit of fear; but of power, and of love, and of a sound mind" (KJV). A measure of spiritual growth is stacking up your pile of fears alongside God's promises. You will find that God has the bigger pile every time.

Spiritual growth is having your hurts healed. I remember, as a little boy, running to my mother after I had fallen and scraped my knee. Mom never yelled and said I should watch more carefully where I was going. She simply bent down, cleaned off the cut, and applied a good dose of iodine. As she bandaged the cut, I was never sure whether the iodine hurt more than the wound itself. She patted me on the head and sent me back to play. The hurt subsided in a few minutes; the bandage stayed for a few days; the scar from the wound stayed forever. You should see my knees.

Healing takes place in our lives when we stop calling attention to our wounds and allow scar tissue to cover them. In the words of Dr. Robert Schuller, "We must turn our scars into stars." James tells us, "Therefore confess your sins to one another, and pray for one another, that you may be healed. The prayer of a righteous man has great power in its effects" (James 5:16).

The healing of our hurts is a sign of spiritual growth. It takes place in the emotional, psychological, and physical areas of our lives. Sometimes it has to start from the inside out. Many of our wounds are on the inside. Internal bleeding is always the most difficult to stop!

Spiritual growth is coming home. Some years ago, I got hooked on a few lines from a song by Chuck Girard. The song was called "Welcome Back." The lines said, "Welcome back to the things that you once believed in. Welcome back to what you knew was right from the start."* I meet many single-again people who, in their journey through life, are coming home to God through their crisis. The crisis of loss is not a place to hide in. It is a place to grow through. God can use your experience to bring you back into a growing place in spiritual things.

Spiritual growth is building or rebuilding your relationship with God. In his book *No Longer Strangers,* Bruce Larson says:

> A right relationship means that one has heard the good news that God says to us in Jesus Christ: "I love you as you are. I love you unconditionally. I have already given myself to you totally, and now all I ask is that you begin to respond to My love and My commitment to you by committing to Me all of yourself that you are able to give."

That is the beginning of building a relationship with God. As in earthly relationships, there is a maintenance program

---

* From the song "Welcome Back" by Chuck Girard, © 1970 Dunamis Music, 8319 Lankershim Blvd., N. Hollywood, Calif. 91605. Used by permission. International copyright secured. All rights reserved.

to be entered upon if the relationship is to grow. I meet Christians every day who have had a vital encounter with God. They joined God's family. They got in the race. They just never traveled very far from the starting line. Then the chaos, the problems, the struggles of life invaded. The question "Why me?" came up. Most often the answer was, "I don't know!" Perhaps a better question is, "How do I grow through this time and come out better for it?"

Building is beginning a new relationship with God. You may need to start your life right there. Rebuilding is coming back to God and continuing the growth you once started, sometimes long ago.

Spiritual growth is coming alive! Can you remember a moment when you felt you were fully alive? It wasn't just because your heart was still beating or because something good had happened to you. It was a special experience that was hard to sum up in human language. But you knew. And you savored that moment.

Those are the mountaintops of our lives. For some of us, it may seem like the valleys outnumber the mountains 100 to 1. Spiritual growth is having a sense of being totally alive in the center of God's love.

John Powell, writing in *Fully Human, Fully Alive,* says there are five things that contribute to one's sense of being fully alive. They are: 1) to accept oneself; 2) to be oneself; 3) to forget oneself in loving; 4) to believe; 5) to belong. To these five I would add one of my own: to minister to others and to be ministered to.

You might take a minute and use the above six as a checklist or a spiritual pulse taking for yourself. Be honest.

If you score low in certain areas, this is where you need to concentrate some of your growth efforts.

Jesus said in John 10:10, ". . . I came that they might have life, and have it abundantly." That sounds to me like being alive. For you it might mean shaking the trappings of another life and life-style from yourself and deciding to get your new life growing! All spiritual growth is measured by daily discipline. That discipline is never easy.

It's like dieting. The first hour is the hardest. The first day is a torment. The first week is agony. Then, all of a sudden, you get in the groove, build up your resistance skills, and just keep moving. The results come slowly at first, then more noticeably. The joy and feeling of being alive comes in seeing the changes.

Then someone throws a pothole in your path in the form of a seven-layer Bavarian chocolate cake—your very favorite. Do you taste the frosting just to see what you were delivered from? Do you have a tiny piece so the cake buyer won't feel offended? Do you eat the whole thing because you deserve a reward for not eating cake for the past eight weeks? We all know that kind of experience: "a tangible temptation of the tastiest variety." It is also a turning point and a place to really measure your growth in dieting.

Steps to Spiritual Growth

There will be some potholes as you grow spiritually. As you come alive, you will find that you are able to handle them easier each time they confront you. I became a Christian when I was about twelve years old. I remember that my Sunday-school teacher and pastor placed more importance on the things I should not do now that I belonged to God than on the things I should do. My list of negatives was long and dangerous. It wasn't until many years later that I realized there was another list—shorter and, for the most part, a lot harder. That list contains things that really help a person grow in his relationship with God. I want to share them with you.

1. *Prayer.* I know, we are starting with one of the hardest ones first. It is no wonder the disciples came to Jesus and said, "Lord, teach us to pray . . ." (Luke 11:1). It's not easy to tell whether they wanted to learn for their own ends or to identify more closely with Jesus. What is implied in their request is that it is a process to be learned. Jesus responded with what is known as the Lord's Prayer. It wasn't to be the only prayer, but it was to be a model, because it summed up what God would want for us. It was a bare-bones, direct-communication prayer. It went from the theological to the practical. The Scripture doesn't say how often the disciples were to pray it. Jesus simply gave the model, and the disciples went from there.

Prayer, simply defined, is a conversation with God about anything. It is also telling God the truth about everything. All of the elements combined in building an earthly relationship go into building a relationship with God in prayer. You have to talk to Him—in twentieth-century English or whatever language you speak.

There are many ingredients that others have written about in discussing prayer that will help you. I just want to find out right here if you are talking to God these days. Are you asking for His help in all of your struggles? Do you have some problems that you feel are too big for God; others that you feel God would not be interested in hearing about? Matthew's Gospel puts it this way:

> "Ask, and it will be given you; seek, and you will find; knock, and it shall be opened to you. For every one who asks receives, and he who seeks finds, and to him who knocks it will be opened."
>
> Matthew 7:7, 8

That's one of God's promises, but we have to do the asking. Prayer is a discipline. It takes time, and it is work. It is the foundation of a growing faith.

2. *Scriptural study.* The four singles crowded into my office. They were excited about the prospect of having a Bible study. We talked about dates, times, and my availability to teach. After we had agreed on these, they turned to go. I stopped them to give a homework assignment prior to the study. Their look of disbelief told me what I had suspected. They wanted me to study the Bible for them and then ladle out the truth for an hour while they listened and then went home. Real Bible study is *you* doing some work—not your preacher or your teacher, but *you.*

The shelves in Christian bookstores are overloaded with study guides, tapes, workbooks, lesson materials, resources, and commentaries. If you are serious about your own growth, you will need to buy several of the tools and get into some study for yourself.

That does not mean you can't go to a study that someone else teaches. It does mean that you can't depend on that as your only study. Just sitting in a room with ten people, reading a segment of Scripture, and then asking what each one thinks is merely a pooling of ignorance, unless you have done your homework. In order to grow, you have to study.

Second Timothy 2:15 says, "Do your best to present yourself to God as one approved, a workman who has no need to be ashamed, rightly handling the word of truth." These were Paul's words to Timothy as he struggled to grow. Are you studying? Do you have the tools you need? Are you in a study group that demands something from you—or are you just being spoon-fed?

3. *Involvement in ministry.* Over the last ten years, I have watched many singles come to a meeting for the first time. They are nervous and unsure about the people, the program, the place, and themselves. Many come once and drift on to some other place. I have discovered that what brings most people back for a second or third time is a reason for them to be there. The strongest one I know is having a responsibility that can only be met by their being present. I have asked more singles to serve coffee than there are coffeepots in California. I have found that coffee servers make great group presidents, social chairmen, and retreat leaders. The beginning of ministry involvement is not as glorious as we would like to think.

Jesus' first request to some potential disciples was simply to "follow me" (Matthew 4:19). That doesn't sound too prestigious. All ministry begins by follower involvement. The tasks come as we are equipped to handle them. I have learned that most people only support what they have a part in creating. Looking for a place to belong is one thing. Having a reason to belong anyplace is another.

Jesus slowly involved the disciples in what He was doing. You need to become involved very slowly in any ministry opportunity. Your desire might be to jump in and take all the reins. Just take one rein. That will give you a reason to be there. Ministry involvement can go from a small group of singles to the larger church body, to mission task forces, to serving as an elder or deacon. There are hundreds of opportunities to serve. You just need one or two to start with.

4. *Fellowship.* As a child, I thought fellowship was food and drink in the church fellowship hall after a meeting. No one really explained to me that fellowship was a lot more involved than that. Fellowship is sharing your life in a supportive community that loves you.

Sometimes when we end a six-week divorce-recovery workshop, the participants ask if they can continue to meet week after week. When told the seminar is over, they usually respond by saying, "I need these people. They have become my friends. I need their support and fellowship." This kind of fellowship comes from people who share the same or similar struggles and experiences.

Fellowship is knowing you are not alone in the human condition. It's having hands to clap for you when you accomplish something. It's having hands to catch you when you falter. It's having your own private cheerleading squad. There is a kind of quiet warmth that comes from deep fellowship with other people. You can hardly explain it, but you certainly know when it's there. The Christian single-again person is in initial fellowship with Christ. That fellowship expands to every other member of the family of God.

5. *The witness of your life.* Paul was standing before King Agrippa. His life was in peril. He was speaking in his own defense. His witness was his life and what had happened to him. He was so convincing that when he concluded, Agrippa said, "In a short time you will persuade me to become a Christian" (*see* Acts 26:28 KJV). Paul was not oratorical. He was not overwhelming. He was not hyperspiritual. He simply told the story of his conversion and his life afterward. The strongest witness anyone can give is to put his life on public display to those around him. Sharing your faith is a big part of spiritual growth. It is taking others behind the scenes to allow them to see what God is doing and has done in your life.

I was finishing a singles conference some months ago on the East Coast. For some unknown reason, a strange thought popped into my head as I was wrapping up the final speaking session. A tape in my mind seemed to keep replaying the words *So what?* I concluded the session by saying, "After all that was said and shared here by so many speakers and myself, I want to close with a question: So what?"

That's what I'm asking you now: So what? What's the difference? Who will make any difference? What about your spiritual growth? Do you care enough in your own life to take some time right now and do some evaluating? No one else can do it for you. Here are some helpful suggestions:

1. Take an honest look at where you are in your spiritual growth and where you would like to be.
2. Make some positive growth plans. Write them down. Put them on your calendar.

3. Be willing to share with others how you are doing and ask their help if you feel you need it.
4. Don't be afraid to take risks and make new commitments to grow.
5. Discover what spiritual gifts you have and find a place to utilize them.
6. Learn to feel yourself spiritually.
7. Watch out for people who set themselves up as spiritual gurus.
8. Don't let others dictate your growth patterns. Spiritual growth is not a race—it's a journey. You don't need to be more "spiritual" than someone else.

My prayer for you is that as you are suddenly single again, you are growing spiritually.

Personal-Growth Questions

(For best results, work with a small group
or one other person.)

1. Write down one area in your spiritual growth that you feel good about.
2. What spiritual-growth areas are you struggling the most with right now?
3. Name one thing that has most profoundly affected your spiritual growth in the past year.
4. What changes has your spiritual growth brought into your life recently?
5. What person do you consider to have helped you the most in your spiritual growth, and why?

7

If Happiness Is Being Single, Why Do These People Look So Sad?

The sleek Datsun sports car raced by me in the fast lane of the freeway. As it disappeared from view, I noted that its license-plate holder bore the slogan "Happiness is being single." I see that slogan every day. Sometimes it's on plain old economy cars, other times on sportier models. I sometimes try to catch a glimpse of the drivers. I want to see if they look happy, and I want to know if that happiness is somehow connected to their singleness.

In speaking to singles audiences over the past years, I have had the opportunity to look into the faces of many singles who wish they were someplace else. Their feeling of unhappiness with singleness is written on their faces. The message seems to be, "Single is the pits."

Many have come up to me after the meeting to say they did not want to be there but a friend had literally yanked them from their hiding places and made them come along. Others have said they were glad they came.

Happiness is not usually going to your first-ever singles meeting as a "single-again adult." Happiness is not usually dispensed at the door as you enter a singles function anywhere in America. Many newly single people expect singles functions to provide them with an instant supply of happiness. The message seems to be, "I'm not very happy. Make me happy!"

Wherever you go, happiness is something you bring with you. You don't go looking for it. You will not find someone to give it to you.

As one lady left our Tuesday-night meeting, she smiled at me and said she was leaving early since there were no men there she was interested in. It wasn't the first time I had heard that kind of comment. What she was really saying was that she wanted to find someone to make her happy and those present were quickly disqualified.

Is happiness a place? Is it a person? Is unhappiness being in the wrong place? Is it being with the wrong person? People and places do contribute to our happiness and our unhappiness. But these are so conditional and variable that they cannot be a true source.

Happiness Hooks

In my work with singles, I hear certain phrases that I think of as "happiness hooks," which give the impression that happiness hinges on one thing, if that one thing would only come about. Let's look at some of those hooks.

If I could just have . . . Mark Twain once said, "If a person had the whole world, he would still want the moon fenced in to shine on his potato patch." What he was saying is that there is no end to wanting. The world of commercial advertising says the same thing. When the automobile was invented and became marketable, the goal was to put one in every garage in America. Several decades later, one is not enough for a family. Now we need one per person. "If I could just have a new one, a better one, a more expensive one, a more sophisticated one." Acquisitions become the rungs on our ladder of success. Society says we need *more!* We have become a society consumed with getting. It is little wonder that we believe happiness is obtaining one more of whatever.

Singles are often led to believe that their happiness would be complete if they could just meet that certain person. Many married people feel they would be happier if they were married to someone else. They leave one person in exchange for another. Divorce easily becomes the unhappiness trade. The high failure rate of second marriages proves that the thing called happiness is not always found in other people. Most often, one set of problems is simply traded for another.

Scores of searching singles float in and out of singles meetings looking for someone to make them happy. How would you like the ominous responsibility of trying to make someone happy? We are all contributors to the happiness of others, but we cannot be the source of another person's happiness. I meet many divorced and widowed people who feel that the happiness they had once known has disappeared with their former spouse. They have decided that they will never be happy again as a single person or that any future form of happiness is contingent upon finding a person to marry.

This was illustrated to me again recently by a young man who sat in my office. He seemed to have his life moving along pretty well as he shared his growth with me. He had experienced a divorce a few years back but had worked hard at rebuilding from the wreckage. I was surprised that his parting comment to me was, "I would be complete now if I could just find the right woman to marry."

Was the young man suggesting he was incomplete because he was not remarried? Many singles I talk with appear to feel this way. Any happiness in their lives seems to hang on finding someone to complete them. God never said *one* was an unhappy number. Being *two* does not necessarily guarantee happiness in anyone's life.

If I could just be . . . When I was twelve, I wanted to be thirteen so that I would be a teenager. When I was thirteen, I wanted to be sixteen so that I could get my driver's license. When I was sixteen, I wanted to be eighteen so that I could be out of high school. When I was eighteen, I wanted to be twenty so that I would be an adult. When I was twenty-one, I wanted to be twenty-five so that my insurance rates would be lower. What a way to go from twelve to twenty-five!

Have you ever based your happiness on being something else? Perhaps you wanted to be younger, older, wiser, richer, thinner, or fatter. Your list could go on indefinitely. The assumption is that we would all be happier if we could just be something that lies beyond our grasp.

There is a great deal of pretense in the world of the newly single. Many singles gatherings are filled with people trying to be something they are not. The assumption is that "you will accept me only if I paint a glowing picture of myself and impress you. If I can gain your acceptance, I will be happy and perhaps you will be happy, also." From time to

time, we all meet people who are playing "Let's pretend."
This is a particular problem in the world of singles.

I have often felt that we should give out buttons at the
doors to singles meetings that simply say, BE YOURSELF! We
all feel most comfortable when we have the freedom to simply be who we really are. Wishing you were something you
are not just robs you of the happiness of being who you are.
Deceiving others locks you into living out a hopeless lie.

Becoming single again does not change who you are on
the inside. Singles who live from the inside out are freer to
share what real happiness is.

If only someone would . . . love me, marry me, make all my
troubles go away, and make me happy. Many of us would
like to rent a person for a day who could do all those things.
Some singles are searching for their own private answer
person who can do it all for them. Stop looking! If you
found one, he or she would only smother you anyway.

Death and divorce bring an endless chain of complica-
tions into a person's life. If you are human, you will have a
few days when you wish the white knight would stop at your
house and take care of everything. The reality is that you
will have to do most, if not all, of your own homework. You
will have days when you feel the gravel of life was all
dumped in your living room. It is ever so tempting to go
looking for someone with a dump truck to haul all that
gravel away for you.

I can recall a beleaguered single mother who sat in my office. She had too many bills to pay, too few hours at home
with her children, too many repairs that needed to be made,

and too little money to make ends meet. Her parting comment was, "I am so tired and overloaded. I wish I could just find some guy with good credit and a steady job to marry me. I'm too worn out to keep going it alone."

I probably hear that kind of conversation at least twice a week in my counseling. "If only someone would rescue me from all my chaos." It's an honest feeling.

I would be a lot happier if . . . We could write almost anything after that kind of statement. Most people, single or married, feel that happiness is "out there" somewhere just waiting to be tapped or trapped. It becomes the elusive butterfly that lingers just beyond our grasp. The problem with this "iffy" happiness is that we are dealing with an unknown. There are no guarantees that we would be any happier than we are now, even if we had everything we had ever dreamed of.

In the eighteenth chapter of the Gospel of Luke, there is an account of a rich young ruler who seemed to have everything. From his conversation with Jesus, it was apparent that the ultimate happiness still evaded him. He had done everything right, yet there was a vacuum in his life. Jesus' response to his query in verse 22 was to sell everything he had and distribute the profits to the less fortunate, and in so doing, he would possess real treasure. This young man, we are told, went away sad, for he had too much to give up. He did not understand Jesus' statement that real happiness comes not from acquiring but from giving.

All of us get caught in acquiring. This often becomes our freeway to success and happiness. The real problem with all this is that real happiness does not come from without. *It comes from within.* Jesus knew that when He tried to unlock the rich young ruler's heart. The scriptural principle is that real happiness doesn't come from being either single or married. It comes from within, as we give ourselves to others. It comes when we help hang a rainbow over someone else's storms.

Dr. Maxwell Maltz, author of *Psycho-Cybernetics,* states that "happiness is internal, produced by ideas, thoughts, and attitudes that can be developed and constructed by an individual's own activities." If what Maltz says is true, then I have to assume personal responsibility for my own happiness. It is centered in my inner being and springs from that into everyday living. I have to look for the source of happiness rather than the manifestations of happiness. As I talk with singles about finding happiness, I make the following suggestions.

Four Keys to Happiness

Put the Creator at the center. Knowing God and experiencing real happiness in one's life go hand in hand. Having God as the center and source of your happiness means that you don't have to rely on external forms of happiness to complete your life. No matter how things go on the outside, there will be a calm and a trust on the inside.

I meet many single-again people across America who have had little religious or church orientation. Some of them ask me how God can be at the center and source of their inner happiness. The answer to that is very simple: *by invitation.* Bringing God into the center of your life happens when you invite Him to take charge of your life and become that inner source of happiness that will not change, regardless of external situations.

The Scriptures tell us, "Therefore, if any one is in Christ, he is a new creation; the old has passed away, behold, the new has come" (2 Corinthians 5:17). I believe that Christ at the center of a person's life is the only key to real happiness. It enables you to live with the quiet confidence of knowing that Someone other than yourself is at the controls of your life. Happiness is knowing that the Creator is at the controls!

Don't try to go it alone with God! Another key to happiness is sharing your life with others who also know God as their source of inner happiness. That doesn't mean you grab your group of Christian friends and head for the hills to start a commune. It means that you live your life in the marketplace but draw special strength and a supportive community from your Christian friends. The Scriptures state that "none of us lives to himself" (Romans 14:7). We draw strength from those concentric circles of relationships that I mentioned previously.

Happiness is being with people who share your faith as well as your struggle. Many of the single-again people I meet are trying to go it alone. They take pride in the fact that they are resourceful and feel that God plus themselves is all the majority they need in life. This certainly was not Jesus' approach. He was a person for others, and those others gave happy meaning to His life on earth. He wrapped His life in significant relationships with the people around Him.

Do the people around you add to your happiness or detract from it? I said earlier that it is not someone else's job to make you happy. However, those around you who are happy will make valuable contributions to your growing happiness.

Give yourself away! A third key to happiness is found in giving yourself away to people who need you. Over the years, I have watched many hurting people who are newly single coming into a singles group for the first time. They are often a collection of bruises and battle scars received in the game of life. Emotionally, many are out of gas. Some just sit and stare and wonder about the singles wasteland into which they have fallen.

After some months, some of the hurts begin to heal, and signs of new life and growth become evident. As the healing progresses, I find many of these people looking for other hurting people whom they can help. A part of anyone's healing process involves helping restore another person to life. Being a people helper, however, is not always easy. Some people will use you in the process. Some will never say thank you, while others will question your motives. Sometimes a person who reaches out to help others can come home at the end of the day feeling like a garbage collector. Many times it is easier to receive help than to give it.

An example of the reward of people helping each other happened recently as a divorce-recovery seminar I was conducting ended. A woman approached me with tears in her eyes and commented on how much help she had received over the past six weeks from the small group experiences she had shared with others in the seminar. My thoughts went back to the first night this group was together and the apparent distrust they had for one another. Now, six weeks later, they had cried, laughed, and struggled together through many of their problems. They had made an investment of themselves in each other's lives and experienced the personal happiness and satisfaction that comes from giving yourself away.

Anyone involved in the people-helping professions will tell you how rewarding caring is and also how tiring it can be. The inner satisfaction of helping another person deepens your own well of happiness.

Learn how to feel good about yourself. A final key to happiness is learning to feel good about yourself. Some time ago, a television commercial appeared featuring a group of young people promoting a soft drink. They were depicted romping down a city street singing the words, "Feeling good about yourself!" The implication was, of course, that you would feel better about yourself if you drank what they were advertising. We all know that happiness is not found in a bottle, whether soda or alcohol.

Feeling good about yourself will greatly enhance your happiness factor. Personal happiness is contagious. On the other side, feeling bad about yourself will send others scurrying from your pathway. Happy people attract happy people. In this area, there are several positive things you can do to improve your self-happiness.

1. *Be good to yourself.* As I stated earlier, I have a friend whose favorite farewell to me is, "Be good to yourself." Usually, I have a hard time with that. It sounds like too much self-indulgence. It is easier to give to others rather than to yourself. But my friend has a point. If you are good to yourself, it makes it that much easier to give to others.

In a sharing session at a workshop, a lady shared how she had given herself a trip to Hawaii when told she should be good to herself. A young man in the same workshop sent a dozen roses to himself at his office. He said he smiled knowingly to himself while everyone at his office speculated where the roses came from.

Single parents often find themselves giving everything to their children because of their feelings of guilt resulting from a divorce. Children, being what they are, just keep on taking, and often give little in return. Single parents need to monitor the giving to be sure they give gifts to themselves.

Even McDonald's, the instant-food specialists, tell us that we "deserve a break today." Apparently too few of us really believe that.

If God's attitude toward us is to give us good things, I think He would be pleased if we were good to ourselves once in a while.

What one thing can you do to be good to yourself in the next week, month, year?

2. *Redecorate and renew your body!* Newspaper and magazine ads tell us it is time to shape up. We all look at the end results of shaping up that are depicted in these ads and wish it could be us, but it sounds too exhausting to think seriously about. We make ourselves a "someday" promise. I have discovered that the feeling of self-worth that comes from shaping my body up is worth the effort and time invested. Every time I finish running a few miles, I am rewarded with a feeling of accomplishment and the knowledge that this is a gift to my body.

How long has it been since you played a sport? rode a bicycle? ran a mile? Don't let your excuse be age and lack of condition. In the Boston Marathon in 1980, the oldest finisher was over seventy years old!

As you renew your body physically, you will find it affirming to do some redecorating in the clothes area, as well. The simple act of buying a new wardrobe can add to your feelings of self-confidence and self-worth. I realize, as you surely do, that an image change may not be an inside change—but it will add greatly to how you feel about yourself.

When was the last time you bought some clothes you liked and enjoyed wearing, even if someone told you that they were "not you"?

3. *Set some achievement goals for yourself!* There is no better feeling in all the world than setting a goal and reaching it. It may be running your first marathon or going back to school for that long-lost degree. It could involve changing jobs, getting your social life in order, or starting that long overdue diet.

The problem for most of us in setting goals is that we want instant attainment. We grow impatient with the process of slowly working toward our goals.

The warm inner feelings of self-accomplishment are summed up in the words of a lady who said, "I'm on my own and I made it," as she waved her new master's degree in my face.

Don't set impossible goals. Set some short-term ones, some mid-term ones, and some long-term ones. The daily, weekly, monthly goals are best to start with. Write them down and cross them off your list when attained. Celebrate reaching them with your friends. Get excited about your accomplishments!

What one goal are you working toward right now? What kind of progress are you making? What are your deadlines for reaching that goal? When you achieve your goal, will you be ready to set even higher goals for yourself?

4. ***Live in anticipation of what God will do in your life.*** I have a little sign on my desk that says, GOD IS UP TO SOMETHING! Some who notice it ask me what I think God is up to. I usually respond by saying, "A million different things in a million different lives." The problem is that God doesn't tell us ahead of time. We live in anticipation of His surprises. That's what makes life exciting. You never quite know what will happen when you give one day at a time to God. He can fill it with challenges that stretch you or serendipities that tumble from your cup of happiness.

In Philippians 1:6 Paul says, "For I am confident of this very thing, that he who began a good work in you will perfect it until the day of Jesus Christ" (paraphrase of KJV). This literally means that God will keep on working in your life, regardless of the circumstances and situations you are going through.

One of America's great writers, Nathaniel Hawthorne, summed up happiness in this way:

Happiness is a butterfly which, when pursued, is always just beyond our grasp, but which, if you will sit down quietly, may alight upon you.

75308

Hawthorne seemed to be saying that the harder we try to attain happiness, the more it avoids us. If we but sit still long enough, we will give it a chance to catch up with us.

What does happiness mean to you? Take a few moments and think through your response. Are you chasing a dream or working on a reality?

Personal-Growth Questions

(For best results, work with a small group
or one other person.)

1. When you think of a happy single-again person, of whom do you think, and why?
2. What one thing do you feel would contribute most to your happiness as a single person?
3. Of all the things I have listed in this chapter to help you feel good about yourself, which one is easiest for you? Which one is hardest?
4. When are you usually the happiest?
5. Is happiness, for you, being single?

8

Unlocking the Fear Syndrome

A woman approached me as the retreat I was conducting came to an end. She began to talk about a move she was considering, from the Midwest to California. As we talked about the excitement of her living in California, I noticed her expression changing from anticipation to fear. Finally, she said she would like to move but was really afraid of a move of this magnitude in her life. I asked her to verbalize her fears. She seemed to put all her fear into one bag with the statement, "I'm afraid I won't make it out there!"

I asked her what would happen if she did not make it and had to return to her present community. She responded by saying that everyone in town would know she had failed.

What was her fear—the fear of new circumstances, the fear of failure, or the fear of what others might think?

All of these are common fears that daily cross the landscape of our lives. We pay such high regard to them that they often immobilize us and keep us from any positive growth and action in our lives.

A single-again person often gets caught between two worlds. One is the world of past failures, and the other is the world of possible future failures. Both seem to squeeze you at a time of important decision making. At this kind of crossroads, it is often easy to make no decisions at all for fear of making the wrong ones.

Recently I asked a group of singles to list the things they feared most. Their responses did not include snakes, spiders, bugs, and assorted members of the opposite sex. Their lists did include such things as being alone, being unsuccessful, failure, rejection, marrying and not marrying, being hurt, finances, and the fear of what others would think about their actions.

If you spend a little time reading your daily newspaper or watching the evening news, you will quickly conclude that the world we live in is filled with fearful things. We walk down our street after dark and are filled with fear as we hear footsteps approaching from behind. We leave the supermarket late at night and double-check to make sure no one is hanging around in the parking lot. Self-defense classes around the country are crowded with people learning how to protect themselves from attackers. Men fear being mugged and robbed. Women fear rape. We all fear a nuclear world war and further economic woes. It is easy to conclude that we have become a fearful society.

Somehow, the outer fears in life seem easier to handle. We can see them, identify them, and respond to them. However, it is the inner fears that will turn into realities. Let's take a closer look at some of the fears that invade our lives.

Fear of Being Unsuccessful

It is every young baseball player's dream to hit a home run with the bases loaded in the bottom of the ninth inning, when his team is losing by three runs. That same dream can turn to ashes if that batter strikes out. The solution for many would be found in the words, "Just don't go to bat or play baseball, and you will never have the problem of striking out." But neither will you ever have the joy of hitting a home run. In every decision in life, there is the dynamic tension of failing or succeeding. We all envy the winners, but no one identifies too closely with the losers.

Many single-again people find themselves locked out of success and achievement because their lives are clouded by past failures. Beginning again says that you cannot change past failures into successes, but you can learn from them. Yesterday's failures should never hamper today's attempts.

A number of years ago, I saw a little sign that explains why some people never reach out to new challenges. The words on the sign were, SOMEBODY SAID IT COULDN'T BE DONE, SO I DIDN'T EVEN TRY! There will be many voices around you telling you to sit still. It is a good thing for you and me that Alexander Graham Bell, Thomas Edison, Henry Ford, and many others tuned out the negative voices of discouragement in their lives. If you have those voices in your life, buy a set of earplugs.

Fear of Failure

This is closely akin to the fear of being unsuccessful. At one time in my own life, the fear of failure kept me out of many new ventures. It was only as I learned that I had the freedom to fail that I began to deal with the problem. As a very young Christian, I was taught that I should never fail at anything. Christians were always winners! Then I began to notice that the Bible was full of accounts of leaders who did not always succeed at what they attempted. Somehow, God still seemed to have a great love for and patience with those leaders. He kept encouraging them and cheering them on. He did not brand them as failures and move on to those with greater possibilities. A short look at the twelve disciples and their struggles would give most of us heart.

Peter and his adventure of walking on the water is an example of the kind of faith it takes to step out of the boat. It also illustrates what it is like to both walk on the water and sink into it. This whole adventure helped Peter grow and learn to risk both success and failure in his growing process.

Are people who try things unsuccessfully failures? I don't believe they are. Our society is often divided into two groups: the winners and the losers. The winners are always rewarded, and the losers are penalized by public opinion and often personal disgrace.

How did Jesus treat people when they failed? He encouraged them! He affirmed them! He loved them! He was not blocked by only seeing what people were or did. He saw what they could become with His help. Peter failed at first in his water-walking adventure. Jesus' words lifted him from apparent drowning.

What would you attempt to do if you knew you could not fail? What is really keeping you from that attempt?

I have listened to people tell me that many singles are

losers. I ask them to define what they mean by "losers."
They usually say that they lost a marriage. But losing a
marriage does not make one a loser in life. The truth is that
we all win some things while losing others.

Failing at something does not mean that you are a failure.
If you fail second-grade math, it does not mean that you are
a math failure for life. Failing at something can be a growing and stretching experience if you go beyond the emotion
to the learning level. The fact that one marriage in your life
has failed does not mean the second one will fail. The key is
to learn from past failures.

Fear of Rejection

Few of us ever learn how to adequately handle rejection.
Many single-again people have told me they became so by
being rejected by their mates for other people. Rejection can
give you a giant injection of poor self-esteem and guilt.
These feelings can clog you up so badly that you never attempt to build new relationships for fear of more rejection.

I am told that some animals have an inborn sense of who
will relate to them in a loving way and who will kick them
out of their path. We humans may be a little behind, but I
suspect that we are catching up. Our antennae are receiving
the signals others send out, and the caution bells are ringing
in our minds. If a rejection is in the wind, we run to safety.

Rejection often starts when we are young. When I was
about six, I would head for the ball field, glove in hand,
ready for a good game of baseball. At that age, I was almost
always the smallest of the guys. When they chose teams,
they usually tried to ignore me or put me so far out in the

field that I couldn't even see home plate. That was only half-bad. When it was our turn at bat, they tried to skip over me because I didn't hit too well. After about seven innings, I usually felt pretty left out and rejected.

I have learned over the years that no one is accepted by everyone. No one has that much charisma or charm. The difference is that many have learned how to handle rejection. One of the surest and best ways to handle rejection is by building your own self-esteem, inner confidence, and belief in your own abilities. If you feel good about yourself, you will not be blown away by how others feel about you. If you are insecure, you will be expecting rejection, and you will probably receive it.

Having people around us who deeply believe in us and our abilities is an aid in dealing with rejection. We all question how good we are until someone else affirms that for us. Their love and affirmation can take us through some rough seas of rejection.

Rejection is also a way to learn. What are the things I am being rejected for? Can I improve on these things in my life? If people stay away from me because I am too shy, I can find a way to conquer shyness. If I am too loud and brassy and people stay at arm's length from me, I can learn how to be more gentle and personable. I can learn from rejection!

Another important way to deal with rejection is to be secure in the knowledge that God will never reject us. Throughout the Scriptures, He tells of His love and acceptance for us. He has promised never to leave us or forsake us. We can be secure in the knowledge that we belong in God's family.

I will have to admit here that some of the members of God's family are not always as accepting as God. Not everyone views us the way God does. God's love for us is not limited by our performance. His love is based on acceptance. When God loves us and we know it, we do not need to fear rejection.

Fear of Marrying Again

For many formerly married people who have gone through a devastating divorce, there is an honest fear about remarrying. The singles world seems to be comprised of two groups of people: There are those who desire remarriage and those who want no part of it.

The biggest fear of remarriage seems to be the fear that it will not work out and another divorce will be imminent. Many people ask me about the guarantees. I wish I could give some, but there aren't any. The wisest counsel I can give is this: Make sure you are really through your divorce and that your life is healthy and growing again. Too many people remarry instantly in order to avoid the emotional whiplash caused by divorce. The pain and hurt are side-stepped, and all the energies are directed toward the new relationship. The problem is that unfinished emotional homework has a way of catching up with you down the road.

Time and the building of trust in a new relationship will remove some of the fears that accompany thoughts of a second marriage. Going to a counselor for premarital testing and counseling is another way to remove the fear. Reading one of the many books that deal with remarriage will also help. (*See* the reading list at the end of the book.)

The fear of remarrying again, like the fear of putting your hand on a hot stove, is a legitimate one and deserves to be carefully considered.

Fear of Not Marrying Again

This fear is tied to the knowledge that a person may remain single for the rest of his or her natural life. It can mean dealing with acute loneliness. It sometimes says that there may not be a "special someone" there to take care of you in your later years, when life and its infirmities catches up with you. Many single-again people list this as their number-one concern. Perhaps this explains the anxiety I often sense at some singles gatherings.

For many people, this anxiety can easily become the "great singles panic." It is somewhat akin to a condition back in my college days that we called the "senior panic." If a girl was not engaged by April of her senior year, she went into a state of panic. Everyone seemed to fear that all the men would disappear after graduation and that all the unmarried girls would be left forever alone.

In an attempt to curb this fear in the singles community, many resort to placing ads in singles newspapers. Still others spend their money on computer matching of men and women. The singles cruises and holiday trips form other ways to deal with this fear.

No one operates well in a state of panic or when surrounded by fear. My observation is that those who seem to worry about it the least and are the most relaxed are the first to remarry. People in a panic do draw a lot of attention. So does a fire. Perhaps a word to the wise would be to slow down just long enough that the right person for you can catch up with you!

Fear of Being Hurt

Most of us have a real fear of physical pain. When we were little and were taken to the dentist for the first time, we wanted to know just one thing: Would it hurt? Many of us were lied to back then and, as a result, we still are trying to escape going to the dentist. He might be the most feared man in your town or your life. You just know that when you go there, you seldom escape without feeling some pain.

Pain is something that most of us spend a great deal of time and money escaping from. When we are told that there is no growth in our lives without some pain, we want to run from the growth. The Scriptures tell us that it is the trying of our faith that brings about patience. Hurt and pain become necessary ingredients in the growth process for all of us.

How do you respond to hurt? Do you harbor it or let it help you grow? To be alive is to risk being hurt. It happens many times a day and in many different ways.

Writing for John Fischer's musical *The New Covenant*, composer Dale Annis graphically portrays what hurt means in these words:

> We all get hurt
> We always seem to end up face down in the dirt.
> And hounded by the pain, we just remain
> Satisfied to be hurt again.

We close our minds
To the meaning in the madness that we find.
We prefer to hide out, rarely try to find out
Just what pain is all about.

But if there's one thing you need to know,
It's that hurtin' only makes you grow.
And the pain you feel
Is the first step in being healed.

Yes, there's one thing you need to do,
It's to get your eyes off you.
Place them on the Lord,
And He'll make pain an open door.

WE ALL GET HURT by Dale Annis
© Copyright 1975 by LEXICON MUSIC, INC. ASCAP
All rights reserved. International copyright secured.
Used by special permission.

In this honest and touching song, we are told the truth
about hurt. We all get hurt, but hurting only helps to make
us grow. Our pain is a healing pain. God uses it as an open
door to our lives. If all our pain were physical, we would
better know how to deal with it. So much of the pain we
carry through life is emotional.

Emotional pain is usually slower to subside than physical
pain. The hurt is inside your heart and head, and it is
usually inflicted by other people. This kind of hurt can stay
around for a long time. It doesn't go away overnight. Often
the path to healing is through forgiveness.

The Scriptures tell us that we are to practice unlimited

forgiveness. Our example for this, of course, is Christ's simple request on the cross, "Father, forgive them; for they know not what they do" (Luke 23:34). Letting go of our hurts through the practice of forgiveness puts us on the road to healing. It also shows us how to deal with the hurts in our lives that are yet to come. Life is a series of hurts and healings. The scars we acquire are simply our badges of growth on the road to maturity.

Fear of Financial Needs

Where will the money come from to pay the rent or buy next week's groceries? What about the doctor bills and the needed car repairs? Few of us live beyond the concern of meeting all of our bills at the end of each month. Financial needs are a very important part of life for the single-again person. Many describe it as the world of "too little of everything that involves money."

Divorce can bring about financial chaos in once-stable families. The death of a mate without adequate insurance benefits can put great financial pressure on a family. The struggle to make ends meet with one wage earner is, at best, precarious. In the tough economic times of the eighties, all of us may be moving rapidly from the age of *more* to the times of *less.* How does the suddenly single person win over this fear?

First, memorize and claim Philippians 4:19. Paul says, "And my God will supply every need of yours according to his riches in glory in Christ Jesus." Notice that this verse talks about needs, not wants. God guarantees that our needs will be met.

Second, talk with your lawyer about your finances. He can

give you a lot of sound advice on what to do with what you have at the moment. He can also assist you in making some long-range plans regarding your finances.

Third, if you need the help of an accountant to put your finances in order, don't hesitate to find one who has done a good job for your friends. Tax laws and structures demand more than just layman's knowledge.

Fourth, sign up for a singles class on finances. Some classes are basic, and some are advanced. Most colleges, junior colleges, and evening schools offer effective and practical courses.

Fifth, read a few good books that deal with the subject. There is a wealth of materials on the market. Buy the practical ones, not the scare-tactic ones that predict financial ruin for the world. (*See* the reading list at the end of the book.)

Finally, learn how to plan and live by a budget. Knowing what you have coming and going through your checkbook can give you a real sense of release and send some of your money fears packing.

Fear of What Others Will Think

In the small-town America of fifty years ago, everyone knew his neighbor. Common problems and joys were public knowledge. It made for a closer community and deeper friendships. Behavior was somewhat modified by the injunction "What will the neighbors think?"

This can be either a safeguard that controls unruly behavior or a deterrent to reaching out for new growth in uncharted areas. In the eighties, we are still between the tension of the two. Much of today's behavior is based on what others will think. Trends, fashions, and fads are all based on being "up" on things so that others will think well of us.

I have listened to singles telling each other what "in" places to go to. If you should go to the wrong singles hangout, others may not think well of you.

Daring to be different and feeling secure within yourself will help you to deal with others' opinions of you. Since you will never be able to please everyone, you might as well stop trying.

Many people spend their whole lives trying to be people pleasers. It starts with trying to please Mom and Dad and win their approval. It carries through to brothers and sisters and the entire family-relative structure. It spills out of the family and into the relationships coming and going in our lives. We even carry it into a marriage and try to recreate the whole cycle in our own families. Sometimes, out of desperation, we scream, "I've gotta be me!" Pleasing people to win their approval never ends, and we can become more and more frustrated.

Many single-again people have discovered that they can be set free from living up to others' expectations. They can break free by simply refusing to worry about other people's opinions and concentrating on developing who they really are and what they want to become.

God and Fear

How does God feel about the fears that bind us and inhibit our growth? In 2 Timothy 1:7, the writer says, "For God hath not given us the spirit of fear; but of power, and of love, and of a sound mind" (KJV). This verse plainly offers an alternative to the many different fears that dominate our lives. It tells us that fear does not come from God. Most of the time it originates within ourselves when we doubt God's ability to do things. Fear captures us daily when we forget that God is still in charge of this universe and all that is going on within it. In place of fear in our lives, God promises us three things.

The first promise is *power.* God gives us power to win the battle against our fears. In the Old and New Testaments, we witness various awesome displays of God's power at work. Some were so convincing that people developed a fear of God. In the New Testament, Paul talks about resurrection power. This is the kind of power that brings life out of death. As we give our fears to God, He gives us new life. We become plugged into the source of fear-removing power!

The second thing God gives us is *love.* It is a key ingredient in His fear-disposal kit. In 1 John 4:18, we read the promise that "perfect love casts out fear." Perfect love is always centered in our love for Christ and His love for us. It was that kind of love that gave Christ the courage to conquer any fear He might have had of the cross. I recently talked with a single man who expressed his own fear of dying. I tried to share with him that Christ had removed even that fear for us by His own death. Death is only a promotion from this life to eternity.

Jesus shared the power of what love could do with His disciples prior to His death. He encouraged them to "love one another" (John 15:17). He knew that His love would bind them not only to Him but to each other. There is great power in the kind of love that keeps us close to one another.

Many single-again people have discovered that kind of love as they share in support groups in singles programs across the country.

The third promise God gives us is a *sound mind.* Did you ever wonder, at the end of the day, if you were going crazy? Perhaps so many strange happenings filled your day and cluttered up your mind that you felt you were losing control. All of us have those kinds of experiences. We start reacting to things instead of acting on things. Our competitive world has a way of squeezing the life juices out of the best of us.

To have a sound mind is to have the mind of Christ in us. It is asking, many times a day, "What would Christ do and say in this setting or situation?" The Scriptures set forth the pattern of how Christ lived and kept His sanity in His day. His ways were usually contrary to the accepted form. The ways of the Christian single person in today's world will still go against the grain.

A sound mind also indicates a mind at peace. How do you even get quiet long enough to have a little peace in this world?

I remember climbing Mount Whitney in the Sierras a number of years ago. The scenery was outstanding. What impressed me the most, next to my sore feet, was the peace and quiet as we rolled into our sleeping bags late at night. It was probably the quietest place I have ever been on this earth.

In His final meeting with the disciples before the Crucifixion, Jesus gave them a gift to carry into the often turbulent days ahead. He said, "Peace I leave with you; my peace

I give to you. . ." (John 14:27). He gave the very quiet of His own soul to the disciples. Perhaps what they failed to realize was that peace is not transferred that easily. It has to be practiced, and they too quickly became preoccupied with the sights and sounds around them.

Are you spending a lot of time perfecting your fear syndromes? Do you solve one and move another one into its place? Are you letting other people aggravate your fears? If you are, you need to let go of the fears. Give them all over to God and let them become His problem. Start moving your life ahead again. Remember, no fear is bigger than God's power to conquer it.

Personal-Growth Questions

(For best results, work with a small group
or one other person.)

1. Write down one of your biggest fears.
2. When was the last time you allowed one of your fears to dictate your behavior?
3. Give an example of how you conquered a fear in your life.
4. How would you tap God's love to displace your fears?
5. How do you feel the people in your supportive community can help you resolve your fears?
6. Express any fears you might have about another marriage.

9

Filling the Potholes

A recent divorce had dropped Barry into the world of the single-again people. As we were talking at the conclusion of a singles conference, I asked him how his life was going. We talked about his task of raising the two children who were placed in his custody. As our conversation concluded, he said that his life was going along pretty smoothly. His only problem was avoiding the potholes in the road of life.

Walking away from our encounter, I began to think about the potholes that litter the suddenly single-again pathway. I reflected on his comment about "avoiding" them and suddenly realized that trying to avoid them would be like trying to dodge raindrops in a thundershower. A better solution would be to try to fill some of those potholes.

What are some of those potholes in the life of the single-again person?

Yesterday's Voices and Memories

You are driving home from work. At a stoplight, you look out the window and spot a tiny French restaurant. Suddenly you burst into tears. You had your twentieth-anniversary dinner there, and your mind flips into reverse and floods you with the memories of that night and the beautiful pearl ring your husband gave you. The rest of your evening is a disaster as you sort through the tears and memories.

I often receive calls from people I have counseled or who have been in my workshops. They share experiences similar to the one above and then ask, "Am I going backward in my growth? Why did I fall apart? Why wasn't I able to handle this?"

All of us are a collection of memories, both good and bad. We have a tendency to let them take over our lives occasionally. Sometimes we hug the good ones and forget the bad ones. Other times we use the bad ones to deter our growth or flood our minds with self-pity. Our lives are like file drawers full of memories. Sometimes the drawers open when we least expect them to and spill our memory files all over us. We remember and laugh, cry, scream, get mad, and go on.

It is easy to feel that when someone has hurt us or wronged us, we should cancel out all the good memories we shared with that person. A healthy person always keeps the good memories in his mental attic. They are to be dusted off and enjoyed at different times. Never let the few bad memories blank out the many good ones. Some people try to do this, and the result is often a frantic search for new relationships from which to build new memories.

A word about bad memories: Don't keep dwelling on them. Bad memories are real bear traps in your thinking and growing. They can cloud your future and cause a lot of rain to fall on your parade through life. Bad memories should be like yesterday's newspapers—read and put away.

Every experience in life is the making of a memory. We sometimes tend to let the bad memories crowd out the good.

A lady recently told me that she had taken permanent care of all her bad memories. She went through the family album with a pair of scissors and proceeded to cut her former spouse out of every family picture. Her feeling was simply, "Out of sight, out of mind." If dealing with our memories were that easy, we would all be in better shape.

We are all a part of one another's memory record. For good or bad, the memories are painted in our minds and imprinted on our hearts. They are part of the contribution to what and who we are today. There is no surgery that will remove them. We simply live with them and learn from them.

Special Times, Special Places

When I was about seven years old, I built my first and only tree house in a large cherry tree on our farm. It was several hundred yards from my home, so it had a certain privacy about it. During my grade-school years, it got a lot of use. It was a special place to retreat to. It housed my dreams and soaked up my tears. I remember years later, visiting my home and climbing up into that old tree and cramming my six-foot-one-inch frame into that small space. I stayed long enough to affirm that this place had been important to me at a special time of my life.

We all have our own tree houses, some real and others imaginary. If life is the making of a memory, then special times and places in our past enrich that memory.

Becoming suddenly single again does not mean the end of special times that were once a part of your life. Many single people seem to have the attitude that their present crisis will cast eternal shadows over their lives. They tend to believe that no experience or person will ever bring special times or places into their lives again.

We make things special by investing ourselves in them. As I had physically and mentally outgrown my old tree house and moved on to my adult life, so many of us need to outgrow the past and go on to the building of some new and very special memories.

Because so many singles treat their situation as temporary, they do no building—or, if they do, it's very makeshift and mobile. Have you ever thought about where you are right now as being a very special time and place for you, or is your primary concern escaping into married territory? Where you are right now can be a very rich and worthwhile place for you. What you build today can be the foundation for tomorrow. Singleness is not an intermission on your road through life. It is a part of your journey. Handle it gently.

You Are Responsible for Making New Memories

Someone has said that the only thing that makes the good old days the good old days is a poor memory. When a person gets older, his time focus seems to shift into reverse. He becomes consumed with all the events of yesterday. Today becomes merely a place to exist. Anything good that ever happened was in the past. The present is denied, and the past is highlighted.

In the last few years of his life, my grandfather became consumed with his past life. I remember his repeated telling of World War I stories and his childhood in England. He never tired of the same stories. The growing infirmities that age brought about only pushed him further into yesterday.

In the Bible, Moses wrestled with memories. He had no sooner gotten the Israelites out of Egypt that they started complaining about the quality of their food. Their memory was filled with the leeks and garlic of Egypt. The manna they were eating day after day simply lacked excitement. They had forgotten the beatings and slavery and the inhumanity forced upon them by the Egyptians. They saw little in their future but a combination of dust and more manna. Their goal of the Promised Land was too distant to embrace. Their thoughts were focused on how good yesterday had been and how bad today was.

From time to time, all of us fall into that kind of trap. Single people are certainly no exception. Like the Israelites, they look for a deliverer. If the deliverer can't deliver for them and help make better memories today than they had yesterday, they become disillusioned.

Who is responsible for making new memories? You are! Not your singles group, not your singles leader, not your relatives and friends. You are! Those around you do become contributors, but you cannot hold them responsible. Too many people wait for others to initiate things that help build new and good memories. Sometimes *you* have to do the reaching out. When was the last time you issued an invitation to someone to join you in building a new memory?

As I look at the sea of faces on the first night of one of my divorce-recovery seminars, I know that those people usually have a giant collection of hurts and bad memories connected to the divorce experience. What a change takes place in six weeks as those same people begin building a new and good memory together. In order for that to happen, each one has to do some reaching out. That kind of experience is often a "memory turnaround" for many people.

Many single-again people who lose a mate by death cling to the memories of their former spouse. Even after remarrying, the former attachments remain. Singles who have remarried someone like this have later shared how hard it was for them to inhabit someone else's memory file and not have the freedom to build new memories.

Memories can be a ball and chain or a rare treasure to be gently handled and kept in a special place. How many new memories have you placed in your file in the past year?

Those Long, Empty Evenings

I once asked a group of newly single people what the toughest time of their day was. The overwhelming response was evenings. Many said that everything went along great until they had to come home at night to either an empty apartment or a single-parent household, with all of its waiting problems. It was then that the reality of being alone hit home. Some even tried to postpone going home until late, so they would not have to face those empty hours until bedtime.

A young businessman illustrated the loneliness he felt at the end of the day by telling me how much he missed having that "special someone" there to recount his day with. He said that two dogs and a parrot did not bring him much companionship, communication, and understanding.

The transition from being married to becoming single again will often mean that there will be no one at home waiting to help you fill empty evenings. If you don't plan to fill your evenings as you fill your days, the emptiness will haunt you.

Look at the creative ways to handle your evenings. An evening class at a local college once or twice a week will give you something to look forward to. Developing a new hobby or two, or taking music lessons, will add to an evening's enjoyment. Planning to read a good book and quietly listen to some good music will make an evening pass rapidly and restfully. Include other people in your plans to fill those empty times. Choose people you enjoy being with.

The greatest struggle to fill those empty hours will be in the first months of new singleness. You quickly realize that you relied on your spouse to make most of the plans for your evenings when you were married. Now, you are doing the programming for yourself. Your toughest task will be to make yourself get going and get doing.

A few single parents have shared their struggle in finding time for themselves in an evening. One mother told me she had no time in the evenings for anything but housework and child work. I asked her if those jobs were planned or just there. Her response was that they were always there and she could never get away from them.

Overloaded evenings can be as bad as empty evenings. Both are a part of being single again. Both demand a plan and a purpose. Both will defeat you unless you are in charge. Don't allow your evenings to be simply potholes between your days!

Weekends

Friday at five, millions of people leave their jobs with T.G.I.F. on their minds. Thanking God it's Friday has become a national pastime for both marrieds and singles. The weekend becomes a time of reprieve and catch-up for all the undone chores and tasks of the week. For many single-again people, it can be the loneliest sixty hours of the week.

If you are a noncustodial parent, the weekend means picking up your children for the visitation ritual. For the custodial parent, it may mean doing all the things that were left undone during the week. For both single parents, weekends can accentuate loneliness and highlight the fact that you have no one to do special things with. Monday morning, when it arrives, seems to be a reprieve from the empty weekend.

Weekends are when most singles groups really move into gear. Trips, parties, and special events are planned to help a person through those often lonely hours. Doing things with other singles will help rebuild your social life. If your weekends have been empty up until right now, start looking for an active and growing singles group in your community that you can join. Don't just be a social spectator—get involved!

I have discovered that many single-again people have done no group entertaining in their homes since their spouses left. Having a group of singles in often unlocks the door to building a new world of friends.

Don't allow yourself to sit at home with your memories. Become a doer. Theater parties, concerts, square dances, hayrides, and maybe even a date are ways to make your weekends exciting.

I meet many very lonely single people. The first question I ask them is whether they have a support group of other singles they do things with. Some do, but many others don't. All of them tell me how difficult it is to attend an event alone when they are used to going to activities with their mates. Well, don't go alone. Call up a few other singles and fill your car. Have dinner together, go to the event, and share your evening.

Find a group you enjoy being with. Make sure they are movers and not squatters. Some singles groups are dead, dead, dead. Someone just forgot to have the funeral. Doing fun things with other singles during the sixty-hour gap will quickly make your weekends times to look forward to.

Holidays

If weekends are bad for some singles, holidays are even worse. Of all of them, Christmas seems to be the worst. My counseling load always escalates in December. Many singles suffer from deep bouts of depression. Others spend their hours calling hot lines in cities across America. Some plan cruises in order to escape the loneliness. Most just grit their teeth and grind through the holiday season.

Holidays are traditionally depicted as family times. Your mind may go back to the special days when you were a child. You find yourself wishing for their return. The first

Christmas without your former spouse is the toughest one. It seems as though the whole experience of the loss of a mate by death or divorce is dramatically highlighted at the Christmas season. The feelings of guilt that arise from not being able to have the other parent there for the sake of the children are devastating. The lack of enough finances to celebrate the season as you once did can cause a blue funk to descend upon you. You can scream about the commercialism of the season, yet feel bad that you can't buy all the gifts you would like to give.

Many single-again people tell me they will not survive the holiday season, but they do.

Sharing Christmas with other singles can be a rewarding experience. They will not take the place of the one you might wish were a part of your celebration, but they will provide a community of love around you at a very special time. Many singles have an open house on Christmas Day and invite others to drop by to share the season with them. Because holidays are people days, opening your heart can add a great measure of warmth to your day.

When you start thinking about being alone at Christmas, think about how Mary and Joseph must have felt as they looked for simple overnight accommodations. The rejection they experienced is identifiable with yours. Their loneliness and frustration are yours. In spite of this, the birth of the King took place.

Most of the other seasonal holidays are survivable. They will be filled with lonely moments only if you allow them to be. You can make the choice of getting lost in the holiday pothole or filling it with people, joy, and celebration.

Birthdays and Anniversaries

These special days in your private life are tough times to live through when you become single again. The days that once called for a celebration now seem to call for a period of mourning. A celebration for one sounds ridiculous, so you plan to ignore the event. Don't! Special times should never die. You should never divorce yourself from them. They are the landmarks by which we measure life. Special times are the hinges on the door to our lives. We need them, and we should plan to celebrate them.

One newly single man told me he made his first birthday after his divorce a giant celebration. He invited old friends and many new single friends. He realized that his life still went on even after a hurtful divorce.

Often the big question of a newly single person is not what to do about his or her own birthday but what to do about the former spouse's birthday. I get asked that quite often. I usually respond by asking people what they want to do.

There are some times in life when we can follow our feelings and not worry about being right or wrong. If you want to send a birthday card to your former spouse, do it. You may not want to throw a party for him, though, unless you have a very unusual postdivorce relationship.

Anniversary celebrations are different from birthdays. An anniversary is a milestone at the end of a year of marriage. When you are no longer married, the milestones end. Don't send cards to your former spouse, and don't sit around feeling bad and remembering all your other anniversaries. File them and find a new way to spend your day. An anniversary is a two-people event. A marriage started it. A divorce or a death ended it. Let the memories stand, but put them away in the back drawer of your filing cabinet and leave them there. You cannot live at the crossroads of those kinds of memories. You must choose to move ahead.

Family Reunions

Staying close to your in-laws after the death of your spouse is usually no problem. You receive love, care, and support from them. You are family, and death seldom changes that. Maintaining a long-term relationship with your in-laws after a divorce can be more difficult. The tension of who is in the right and who is in the wrong often becomes a family game. Sometimes you feel as though the teams are choosing sides and you are in the middle. If you have children, the grandparent relationship can become one of tension. If your ex-spouse remarries, you may find your in-laws' allegiance switching to his or her new mate.

Some divorced people have told me they still are invited to all family events given by their in-laws. They attend even if their ex-spouse is present with a new mate. I think the important thing is to decide what kind of relationship you would like to have with in-laws and then go after it. By the same token, your parents are in-laws to your ex, and he or she has the right to pursue a relationship with them, even if you don't like it. A divorce causes many breakdowns in family-relative structures. A remarriage can also bring you into another structure that is far from loving and stable. These are often the offshoots of divorce that no one ever thinks about until they happen.

Both death and divorce eventually cause a shifting of family ties. Being family to someone can be and should be more than just a blood or marriage tie. It need not end just because you are single again.

The single-again life is filled with many potholes. You can choose to get lost and buried in them, or you can climb out of them, steer around them, and move your life ahead. There are no guaranteed answers to the many potholes I have shared in this chapter. You simply try things that have a possibility of working in the different situations I have mentioned. You ask those around you what kinds of answers they have found in working through the difficult places. Then you take the creative risks that will help you live on the growing edge of your new single life.

Personal-Growth Questions

(For best results, work with a small group
or one other person.)

1. How well do you feel you are doing at filing yesterday's memories?
2. What is the toughest special event for you to deal with as a single-again person?
3. How did you handle your first Christmas alone? If it is still in the future, how do you see yourself handling it?
4. What particular potholes are you having trouble filling right now?
5. Describe your current relationship with your in-laws.

10

New Career Beginnings

Newly divorced and fifty-three years old, she stopped by my office on her way home from the employment agency. Amid a sea of tears and a deeply crushed spirit, she told me of her two-hour ordeal trying to find a job. After she had answered many questions and filled out a blizzard of paperwork, the counselor informed her that she had no marketable skills and would probably have to go back to school in order to obtain some training for the job openings available.

In the past ten years of working with newly single people, I have listened to this story hundreds of times. The only variable is the age of the applicant. The response is usually the same. The reality is that the world is not waiting to hire women who are suddenly single again through the death or divorce of a mate.

A vast number of women affected by divorce must find a way to survive economically in an already overloaded job market. Many of them have been out of the work force for twenty to thirty years. The fact that you worked in a library when you were twenty-two has little bearing on job economics in the eighties. Many women dust off a twenty-year-old degree in sociology or English, only to find out that today's more skilled graduates form a long line in front of them. It is easy for the lines of discouragement to form a circle around your worst fears.

A number of people I have met have switched from the employment line to the welfare line. Their despair at losing a mate is compounded by their despair at not finding meaningful employment. Beginning again in the working world is no easy task. The few who have worked during their marriages are least affected. They simply continue on. The others often end up with meaningless and mundane jobs simply to have a few dollars coming in. Still others are convinced they will never find a decent job, and their pursuit switches to finding someone who will support them so that they will not have to work.

Becoming single again at any age means many new beginnings in your life. Few things stay as they once were. Some of those changes can be welcome adventures in new growth. One such area is your career.

Keeping On

Many people already have very satisfying jobs when they find themselves suddenly single again. The job may be so satisfying that they try to hide in it during their period of loss. Their former eight-hour day becomes a sixteen-hour day with overtime on weekends included. They feel that drowning themselves in their work will keep the pain away. My feeling is that many men try to deal with their emotional upsets this way. A few women might do the same thing.

Work can become an obsession. It can also seem to be the

only area in which you have any control over your life. A lack of achievement in family life and marriage can mean a frantic rush to gain some measurable success in your job.

On the other hand, keeping on in your present work can be a good form of therapy. It can take your mind off some of the problems that cannot be solved today. It can fill potentially empty time, and create a sense of fulfillment and self-worth.

Changing

When many things are changing around you, some by choice and some by chance, it gives you the opportunity for a total reevaluation of every area in your life. One of the areas that many people look at last is the career area. Somehow, you feel that this area is too sacred to tamper with or evaluate. Or your fear of making changes drives you back to the security of leaving things as they are. One of the positive things that comes with becoming single again is the opportunity to take a long look at your job, career, or vocation, and ask yourself the question "Is this really what I want to do?" I will admit, this is a risky question for everyone, single or married.

Several years ago, I asked that question myself. The answer produced some profound changes in my own life that moved me from the security of a church ministry to a national traveling and speaking ministry. I also discovered that you will run into two types of people when you make this kind of drastic change in your life.

The first type of person questions your change and tells you that he or she would not have done it if they had the choice. They dredge up a long list of fears, and finally tell you that they simply can't understand how you could do that kind of thing. They are the discouragers!

The second type of person is the one who, when told of your change, tells you how excited he is for you and affirms your decision in every way. He is an encourager! We all need lots of this variety in our lives, and as few as possible of the first variety. Too many people, while reevaluating a career decision, go from person to person in a "pooling of ignorance" routine. They ask everyone's opinion and either do nothing or do what the last person they were with told them to do.

Sound and trusted counsel and input is always valuable, while a collection of opinions just confuses the issue. There are several questions I have used numerous times in my life when I am faced with evaluating changes. Get a pencil and answer these for yourself. It could mean the beginning of some changes in your career.

1. *Why are you doing what you are now doing?* Sometimes when I travel, I use this question in getting to know the people who pick me up at the airport. I usually ask them first what they do in their job. They respond easily to that. When I follow it with a "Why do you do that?" question, I sometimes get a confused look. Some respond by saying, "I've always done that." Others tell me that they were trained for that specific job years ago. Still others tell me that their family has been doing that certain job for over a hundred years.

I am sure that all of these responses are very legitimate. I am not sure that they are always valid. Many people today are leaving jobs and careers that they were trained for, and are starting over. Sometimes the challenge is gone and the career becomes a sentence that will only be relieved by death. I meet many people who are extremely unhappy with their jobs. I wonder why they continue to do them. Fear of change? Fear of what others will think? Fear of failure? Fear of financial loss? Fear of success? Probably a little of each.

Some people get into jobs temporarily, until something else comes along. Nothing new comes crashing through the door, and they simply settle into a rut after a time. They can wake up ten years later with a locked-in feeling, wondering how they got there in the first place. If you take a job temporarily, keep reminding yourself of that. That job is simply a passageway to the next part of your journey.

2. *Are you happy and fulfilled in what you are doing?* We spend many hours during a lifetime at our employment. If our work is exciting, rewarding, and challenging, we will be fulfilled. If it is a dull and weary experience, we will have a lot of misery. That misery will carry over into every other area of our lives. It will affect our families, children, relationships, and our own physical and mental health.

Happiness in a job is being happy while you are doing it and being happy with the results that come out of your job. It is doing the job well and meeting new challenges as you do it. When the challenge goes out of a job, boredom sets in. Weekends and holidays become release and relief from the job. What is there about your job that makes you happy right now? Take your pencil and continue the list.

3. *Is your present job the best investment of your abilities and talents?* Each of us brings to any task in life a vast assortment of the abilities we possess. Some of those tasks call forth a wide variety of what we have. Others need very little. Unused abilities and talents get rusty and decay. Only the talents we call up to use stay sharp and honed. As they are used increasingly, they become perfected. When was the last time you listed all of your abilities and talents? Have you had your close friends confirm those things you see in yourself as well as what they see in you?

One of the best ways to identify your own gifts is to have others call them out of you. It is the little-league coach who watches a new player swing the bat with confidence and natural ease. He sees in him the power to be a hitter. He views him on a major-league team down the road. His job is to call that gift out and affirm it. Some people are doing jobs and are locked in careers that either misuse their abilities or don't use them at all. Your personal satisfaction and happiness will be at stake if you are in a position that does not use your abilities to their fullest.

The world has a lot of people in the wrong places. The key is that you don't have to stay in the wrong place. You can move and change and make steps toward where you want to be. Take your pencil out again and list your gifts, talents, and abilities. Are you using them in your present job or career?

4. *What would you rather do right now than what you are doing?* If I left a blank space right here, I think I know the first thing many of you would write. Retire! Go to Hawaii or the South Seas to live! Never work again!

I lived in Florida for a number of years, and I used to watch the endless migration of retirees who finally accumulated enough years at their occupations to get the gold watch and retire to a neat mobile-home park in the sun. For the first months, they bragged that this really was the way to go. After the initial excitement wore off, they started looking around for something meaningful to do with their time. Few seemed to find it. Many started drinking more heavily as a release from their boredom.

Some things appear to be what we want, until we get them in our grasp. It's like the child who wants many new toys and gifts for Christmas, and ends the day playing with the empty boxes they came in. Asking the above question is not intended to send you on a flight into fantasy. It is to help you look at other viable options for your life. Some people have dropped their lifelong careers and turned their satisfying hobbies into jobs. If you get more satisfaction and fulfillment from your hobby than your career, perhaps you should think about this kind of change.

Martha is a good example of a single-again person who made a hobby-to-career change. Her hobby was refurbishing old houses that were run down and unsalable. She started buying these little ramshackle places that nobody wanted. In a few short months, with her deft decorating skills, the houses were transformed and sold, often on the first day of their listing.

Martha slowly moved along with buying, renovating, and reselling until before long her hobby employed many others who worked along with her. She often had four or five houses under repair at the same time. Soon she was buying larger and more expensive homes and giving them the same treatment. When I last spoke to her, she had built a whole empire in the real-estate world and had hired a property manager to keep track of all her holdings. Martha had made the giant leap from a fun hobby to a prosperous career.

I have had some single-again people tell me that their job or career is their joy in life and they would rather do that than anything else. That's usually a good test of the above question. If you would rather do nothing else than what you are currently doing, you are probably being fulfilled in your present situation—either that or you are making too much money to change to what you really want to do. Take a minute and list your "rathers." Are some of them feasible for you? What would it take to accomplish them? Do you find yourself getting excited at the possibilities?

5. *What did you want to do when you were a child?* Most parents ask their children what they want to be when they grow up. If they want to be in a prestigious profession, the parents then brag to everyone within earshot that their Johnny or Mary is going to be a doctor, lawyer, and so forth, when they grow up. Some children grow up with their pre-cast careers taking shape around them. To follow any other would be a grave disappointment to their parents and fellowman.

Many little boys who won speech contests in school were told by their parents that they would be great preachers someday. Thirty years later, they found themselves in a career that they were ill equipped to handle in areas other than speech. Childhood is a time to dream great dreams of tomorrow. For some of us, those dreams become obstacles that prevent us from doing what we really want to do. For others, the dreams were forgotten for more realistic pursuits. I am not so sure that the things we showed great interest in as children should have passed away as we matured.

Being single again can be a time to think through some of those dreams and perhaps begin their pursuit. It was not until my father's death that my mother was able to pursue her childhood dream of becoming a nurse. For a number of years prior to her death, she was able to do something she had always wanted to do. Many children abandon their dreams because they are told by ill-informed parents that they are too stupid, too small, too unathletic, too poor in math, and so on. Many newly divorced people have told me that they had been convinced by their spouses over the years that they could not do certain things, only to find out after the divorce that this was untrue. Many of us will never grow up. We will be changing, growing, trying, and thinking new things throughout life.

Starting Over

Moving ahead and making changes accounts for a certain segment of the newly single-again population. These are people who are in jobs and careers or who are changing from one thing they have been doing to another they desire. What about the mother with three children and fourteen years of housewifing to her credit? With the death or divorce of a mate, the economic situation in one's life changes rapidly. In many homes, the mother has to seek employment. With few up-to-date skills, where does she go and what does she do?

Most major colleges and universities across America have added women's departments to their programs. One such program in our area is called "Reentry Options for

Women." It deals with bringing a nonworking woman into the work force. It is not an employment agency. It goes well beyond that, as it attempts to interview, test, and educate women to what is available.

The job market of twenty years ago is vastly different from that of today. Many jobs that existed then are obsolete today. Even your college major may be obsolete. New jobs and career opportunities are being born every day. Many are looking for people. Most people don't know they exist.

The old myth that a woman must take a "servant" position or job is long gone. Women, over the past ten years, have obtained positions in the executive world once dominated by men. The accomplishments of the women's movement in the seventies will update many single women on the progress that has been made.

Educational opportunities abound. The listing of evening adult-education classes offered by the colleges in my own area is incredible. Training is available for every conceivable career or job. Classes are held at convenient hours. Many are free while others have reasonable charges. Perhaps the greatest fear a woman has in looking into a new career or even a first career is that her choice will be wrong. Don't let that deter you. You have the freedom to test the waters and move on to another situation if you choose to. There is nothing that says you have to be stuck in one career just because you started it. That kind of thinking becomes a trap to growth.

Another thing to be wary of is being sold on a certain field of employment because there are numerous openings or because the field offers great security. Neither of these aspects will mean much to you if you are unhappy with what you are doing. You need to do your own homework and make sure that you want to try a certain area. Don't let others talk you into something you really don't want to do.

Have you done your homework yet? Drop by your local college or university. Check out what it has to offer. Take the testing program. Sign up for a course or two. Investigate all the opportunities. Let yourself get excited!

Waiting to Be Rescued

A little earlier in the chapter, I mentioned a group of people who look around for someone to support them so they won't have to face some of the things I have talked about. Waiting to be rescued from singleness is deadly. First, you will never know whether you had what it takes to be responsible for your own life. Second, your knight in white may deliver you from employment and its frustrations but bring far more hazardous problems into your life.

Many single-again people are willing to make a trade-off in this area. I am never quite sure that they understand what they can lose. I cannot stress enough the feelings of self-confidence, self-worth, and self-accomplishment that come from the new beginnings of career development.

New Careers and Jobs for Men

Divorce usually means that women have to enter the work force. What about the changes for men? Many continue to do what they have always done. Others use the single-again time to evaluate where they are vocationally in their own lives. Some men choose to move to new areas of the country after a divorce or the death of a mate. They want to experience new memories and new beginnings. Still others go back to school for further education. A few decide to change to another field of work. As one man recently shared with me, "I've always been in the career my wife wanted me to be in. Now I am going to do what I want to do for the first time. I'm going to manage a resort." Both men and women have found themselves in occupations that were prescribed by others in their lives. When those others no longer have control, there is a freeing of the spirit to attempt new things.

Too Old and Tired?

I frequently speak with single-again people who are over sixty. When they hear me talking about new jobs and developing new interests, they sigh and tell me that they are too old and too tired to attempt anything. I am always amazed because as I read the Bible I find that God really doesn't seem to care much about age. Retirement is not mentioned in the Scriptures. Moses was well into his eighties when he undertook his greatest leadership assignment.

In today's world, Colonel Sanders and Grandma Moses were apparently late bloomers. Their success came well after age sixty-five. Many older singles seem content to serve time. Their unhappiness and lethargy is largely due to their lack of motivation and belief in themselves. Age has nothing to do with growth. New opportunities come to open minds and open hearts.

New Road Ahead

If you are past the crisis of losing a mate by death or divorce, it's time to start looking at your future. It is in your hands. Don't get locked in a holding pattern. Spend some time alone asking yourself some hard questions about your vocational tomorrows. Get with some trusted resource people and let them help you. Start planning for yourself. Take some of the little steps that will get you going. Celebrate your progress! You are on a new road!

Personal-Growth Questions

(For best results, work with a small group
or one other person.)

1. Why are you working at the job or career you presently have?
2. Where would you like to be and what would you like to be doing two years from now? five years from now?
3. How do you feel about starting over in a new field or vocation?
4. Have you ever refused a job because you were afraid to fail? Describe what happened.
5. Write down some of your vocational goals for the next five years.

11

Catch the Serendipity Spirit!

The story is told about the three Princes of Serendip. In the black of night, they were riding their camels across the desert on a journey. Suddenly, a voice from nowhere told them to dismount, reach to the ground, and pick up what they found lying there. The voice informed them that when daylight came, they could inspect what they had picked up. It also told them that they would be both happy and sad at their discovery.

When the light dawned, they reached into their pockets and discovered that they had picked up a handful of precious gems. They were happy that they had taken as many as they did but sad that they had not taken more.

Catching the serendipity spirit in your life is making the same discovery as the three princes. Being single at this point in your life can be a serendipity experience for you. You have a choice to pick up the many things that will enrich your life while you are single. They may not appear to be dazzling jewels to you right now, but down the road a way, you might be amazed at what you possess.

In this chapter, I want to share some of the serendipities

connected with singleness. But to help you really appreciate those serendipities, first let's take a few minutes and look at attitudes toward singleness.

1. *Fear of singleness.* Are you living with all the fears that being single can bring into your life? I said in an earlier chapter that fear can immoblize a person. Many people are so afraid of all the things they have heard about singleness that they simply want to run away and hide from it. The things we fear most seldom happen to us. Fears are dissolved when discoveries are made.

A lady once told me that she had tried to come to my singles group for three consecutive weeks. Her fear never let her get out of her car in the parking lot. She drove in, drove around, and drove out for three weeks. On the fourth week, she parked but sat in her car, afraid to go in the door. Just as she was about to start her car up and pull out, a lady tapped on the window and invited her to go into the meeting. She probably would not have made it to this day if a caring person had not noticed her fear. Her final comment to me was, "I really enjoyed tonight. I don't understand what I was afraid of." What are your greatest fears of singleness? Maybe you are fighting a paper dragon.

2. *Hurting in singleness.* Are the hurts that you acquired in your marriage carrying over into your singleness? Some single-again people who have experienced a divorce spend all of their physical and mental energies trying to get even with a former spouse. They have been hurt, and now they want to hurt in return. Other hurts come from the people around you who don't understand your situation. They judge, condemn, indict, and you are wounded.

Another hurt comes from the guilt you place upon yourself. You seem to absorb this inwardly, but the results are manifested outwardly. It is easy to spend a great deal of time licking wounds and buying bandages. Sometimes it takes more human energy to remain hurt than to let those hurts heal.

In divorce-recovery seminars, I watch as people let go of their hurts through the process of forgiveness. I see anger and pain replaced by a smile. It is a process, and it begins with the decision not to hug your hurts any longer. Are you keeping your hurts at the top of your list? Are you looking for vengeance? Clutching your hurt will only rob you of healing.

3. *Adjusting to singleness.* Adjusting to new life situations is like buying a new pair of shoes. The old ones are always more comfortable but somewhat less respectable in appearance. The new ones are stiff and squeaky and usually uncomfortable for a time. This will change once they have been worn and broken in. It's not an overnight experience. It means not taking relationships for granted.

Many people take each other for granted during marriage. You cannot carry this attitude into the singles world. Having to face what I sometimes call "second adolescence" makes single-again people feel as though they have been placed in a time capsule and shot backward to their youth. The pressures of dating and relating to members of the opposite sex again can prompt you to scream, *"Foul!"* A sense of unfairness and a "Why me?" attitude can consume a lot of your mental energies if you are not on guard. Are you willing to adjust slowly to your new singleness? Are you willing to take time and trust the experience?

4. *Accepting singleness.* Accepting singleness usually starts in the mind. It may be admitting that this is not where you planned to be or even wanted to be at this time of your life. You may, in fact, not even like being single. Accepting it is knowing that whatever you think and feel, being where you are is a reality for right now. I counsel many single-again people to cultivate the habit of saying, when asked, that they are *single now!* That does not mean forever. It means for now. I meet some newly single people who seem to have accepted singleness as a permanent form of punishment in their lives.

You can only face singleness if you are willing. Some new singles try to hide out with married people. They feel secure with them and can pretend that they, too, are still married. That's not healthy. It's a game you will ultimately lose. As you accept singleness, you will find that world populated with some of the nicest people you have ever met. Are you accepting or denying where you are?

5. *Trying to escape singleness by marriage.* When people lose a mate either by death or divorce, they often find themselves extremely vulnerable emotionally. They become very susceptible to any form of caring or attention coming from the opposite sex. It is easy to confuse caring and loving. I watch many single people marry someone who cared when they were hurting. A few months into the new marriage, they may find they have very little in common. Often, a second divorce will occur within a year or two of that marriage. Many of these second marriages that fail are simply emotional collisions.

Other singles try to remarry quickly in order to get even with their ex-spouses and prove that they can catch someone. Still others are so afraid of being alone in life that they will attach themselves to any warm body. Are you looking for an easy exit from singleness? If you are, you will probably find one. Look out! It may be a dead end.

6. *Enjoying singleness.* There is an initial period of chaos and confusion in the life of every single-again person. People arrive at singleness by different routes. Some who have lived in deteriorating marriages look upon singleness with relief. Others who were happy in their marriages look upon it with fear. It takes a year or two to put the past behind you and begin to build new memories. There will be a day down the road when you will look around at where you have been. Then you will look at where you are and where you are headed and stop just long enough to give yourself a cheer. Part of your joy will be at knowing how much you have grown. The other part will be at the excitement of what is ahead of you.

A tremendous strain is lifted from your shoulders when you can begin to feel good about where you are now and know that you no longer have to look for a quick out. I meet many single men and women who are really enjoying every aspect of their singleness. As one very meticulous man said, "When you come home to your apartment at night, you find everything just as you left it. If you can't find something, then *you* misplaced it."

Now that you have taken an honest look at your attitude, let's go on to serendipities.

Freedom of Choice

In marriage, your freedom of choice is sometimes restricted dramatically by either the dominance or dependence of your mate. Your life can become a computer card deposited each day in your matrimonial computer. Your program can be written by your spouse, and you merely perform what is planned for you. Your choices can be limited and your joys few. Becoming single again often sets a person free from that kind of stifling control. Initial freedom from that kind of bondage can make you very uncertain. Programmed people are performers. People who are not programmed have to learn to initiate things for themselves.

The myriad number of choices in the new single life are often very confusing. There are sometimes too many too soon. You wonder if you are making the right decisions or the wrong ones. Don't forget, I said earlier that you have the freedom to fail. Making choices for yourself is both liberating and frightening.

Take a few minutes right here and make a list of the choices you can make in the different areas of your life as a single person. I'll suggest a few; you add yours.

> You can eat any kind of food you like.
> You can eat anytime you want.
> You can live anywhere you choose.
> You can work at anything you like.

I just noticed that you were looking around trying to find someone to give you permission to do the above. *Give yourself permission!*

One lady told me she was going to become a mechanic after her divorce was final. She said she had always wanted to tinker around with cars, but her husband told her it wasn't ladylike and she would get greasy and dirty. She no longer needed his consent.

You can live where you want and how you want. Maybe you lived with Mr. or Mrs. Clean all your life. Now you can leave the newspaper on the floor once in a while.

A lady approached me at the end of a workshop and invited me to come to the parking lot to see her new car. She was a quiet, reserved, gray-haired woman of about forty-five. I had a mental picture of a nice conservative Ford or Chevrolet four-door in a deep maroon color. We walked past about three of those. Then she pointed to her car, sitting alone in the corner of the lot. It was a bright blue and white Mustang with racing stripes, air scoops, spoilers, mag wheels, sun roof, custom stereo, and a giant whip antenna. My shock made her smile as she told me why she bought it. That's right, you guessed it: twenty years of driving the cars her husband chose. Nice, quiet, conservative cars. Finally, she had the freedom to choose something she had always wanted. Second adolescence, you say? No. Simply a person who wanted to make her own decisions once in a while.

The adventure of a new career is another choice that is often denied within the structure of a marriage. I have witnessed people literally coming alive with excitement as they made their own choices in this area. The choices are there for you to make. They are limitless. Take the risk.

There are some lines of free verse someone has written that describe taking risks.

To laugh is to risk appearing the fool.
To weep is to risk appearing sentimental.
To reach out for another is to risk involvement.
To expose feelings is to risk exposing your true self.
To place your ideas, your dreams, before the crowd is to risk their loss.
To love is to risk not being loved in return.
To live is to risk dying.
To hope is to risk despair.
To try is to risk failure.
But risks must be taken, because the greatest hazard in life is to risk nothing.
The person who risks nothing, does nothing, has nothing and is nothing.
He may avoid suffering and sorrow.
But simply cannot learn, feel, change, grow, love and live.
Chained by his certitudes, he is a slave.
He has forfeited freedom.
ONLY A PERSON WHO RISKS IS FREE!

You Don't Have to Ask Permission

I remember how embarrassed I used to get in elementary school when I had to raise my hand and get permission to go to the washroom during class. I wished many times that I could just sneak out and sneak back. Most of us learned back then that life is an endless series of having to ask permission. You simply cannot live and do your own thing at the expense of others.

There is, however, a fine line between freedom and enslavement in doing things. Many formerly married singles still feel they have to ask their former spouses' permission to do certain things. They say they have a hard time with their new freedom. Others admit that initially they did not mind asking their spouses for permission to do certain things. What bothered them was that this soon turned into restrictiveness and a lack of freedom imposed upon them by their mates. Many were belittled and put down for so long within their marriages that they simply became subservient to their spouses.

Being single again means that you can give yourself permission to do something. You don't have to ask others if it is all right. Those choices I just talked about are really yours. There is a poem titled "Ambivalence" that I often share with people in my workshops. One of the key lines says, "I give myself permission to change in the way I think best and not box myself in with the expectations of others, to learn to be my own person and not forever live in the past." You have permission—yours! What changes need to be made in your life?

You're Not Owned by Anyone

The bridegroom was walking around greeting guests at his wedding reception. As he talked with another couple, I overheard him say, "Well, she's mine now!" As he said it, he hugged his wife to his side. At that moment, his wife probably felt good about the comment and didn't give it a second thought. Ten years later, that same comment could become a noose around her neck.

Marriage is not ownership. There is a fine line between being owned and belonging. Many men and women have the idea that marriage creates an ownership of another person.

There are three kinds of relationships in a marriage. *Dependence* is the kind of a relationship where one person leans on and counts on the other person to meet all his or her needs. *Independence* is a relationship where each person operates on his own and only works with his spouse when necessary. *Interdependence* is a shared relationship of two people in all the things that a marriage can be.

Many marriages that end in divorce were ownership relationships. One mate felt the other person was his or her personal property. That can create a dependency factor in the newly single person, or it can create a disdain for getting close to anyone again. Many singles live in reaction to former ownership by loudly telling everyone that they are their own person. This response usually drives people away from them.

Being your own person means you want to be allowed the space you need to reach out and grow. Your life, in or out of marriage, is always a shared existence. You have a good, sound mind that can make choices and decisions. If anyone has to own you, let it be God. The great thing about having God in your life is that He lets you make choices. He simply promises to be your Friend and give you guidance.

You Set Your Own Priorities

I sat down the other day and made a long list of things I had to do in the upcoming week. Maybe you did the same. As the list got longer, I became more panicky, wondering how I would get everything done. That's about the point that I usually start worrying, and then I slowly become numb and resort to some extracurricular activity that is not on the list but delivers me from having to confront reality.

Wisdom would have me go over the list and put a 1 beside all the things that are priorities and must be done, then a 2 beside others, and a 3 or 4 beside the rest. We have all seen the little sign in someone else's office: THE DIFFICULT WE DO RIGHT AWAY, THE IMPOSSIBLE TAKES A LITTLE LONGER!

Learning to sort out your priorities is a lifetime process. It demands constant attention and reevaluation. Life is such that your priorities collide with the priorities of others. Anyone in leadership knows how difficult it is to sell your list to those who work under you. What is important to you invariably will be in second or third place to them. Another factor is that priorities constantly change. The spotlessly clean house you once took pride in somehow seems less important now. The rules and regulations that you imposed upon yourself and others may seem rather insignificant now that your situation has changed.

There is a growing list of services for busy people. I recently read of a service that will come to your home and help organize your personal closet and wardrobe. That sounds exciting to me, yet my fear is that I will end up being programmed by someone else. Some days I would welcome that, on others, never. I am responsible for my life, and I must set my own priorities. Many single people whom I meet struggle in this area. Their priorities are jumbled by the people passing in and out of their lives.

What are your priorities? Can you spend a few minutes right now and make a list? Rate them in the order of importance in your life. Then, after you have worked on your list for a while, evaluate how much time you are giving to those varied priorities. It might even be a good idea to make a list of your priorities before you became single again, and compare it to your list now. Once you have done this, know that it's not a once-and-for-all experience. Revision, updating, and reorienting are an ongoing process.

How many of your priorities are dictated by someone else? Getting in charge of your own life again means some of those priorities must be *yours.* Here are some of the common priorities I hear in counseling newly single people.

1. *Personal time.* You need time just for you to do what you want to do. Read, sleep, rake leaves, ride a merry-go-round, walk in the rain, read poetry, window shop, see a friend.

2. *Children.* Many newly single persons are also newly single parents. Raising children with both parents in the home is tough. Doing it by yourself is super tough. Your children need quality time from you. You need quality time from them.

3. *Job.* Does it run your entire life? Are you able to keep it in perspective to your other responsibilities? Do you take it home with you in the evening and on weekends? Is it causing you more unhappiness than happiness?

4. *Social life*. Do you have any leftover energies and time to be involved with other singles socially? Do you set apart special time on your weekly calendar for this outlet? Are you building a new circle of single friendships?

Sometimes when we get overcrowded with our long lists of things and priorities, a good question to ask is, "A thousand years from now, will this really matter?" If you want to be more realistic, will it even matter next month? Becoming suddenly single again means that you are responsible to set your priorities. No one else should be allowed to do it for you.

How to Experience a Serendipity

We have all gone to various events in our lives that we predicted would be dull, boring, uneventful, and a waste of time. Periodically, one of them becomes a serendipity. We expect one thing and are quite surprised by another. We go away acknowledging how happy we were to have been present.

Look for the small serendipities in life. Maybe the party you attended did not live up to your expectations, but the super person you met there made the evening shine. Sometimes a simple, affirming conversation with another person becomes a special event. Serendipities are sprinkled throughout life. Most of us spend too much time looking for the big ones and miss all the little ones. Expect them to happen to you, and they will. When they do happen, celebrate them!

Learn to be a giver of serendipities. You may make someone's day by sending him a card of encouragement. Giving a warm hug can make a day take on a whole new gleam. A telephone call to a cross-country friend can be something special to him or her. In order to be a receiver of serendipities, you have to be a giver of them. You can't just collect them and hide them away.

Someone has said that love isn't love at all until you give it away. You are in a special place in your life. Catch the Serendipity Spirit!

Personal-Growth Questions

(For best results, work with a small group
or one other person.)

1. Of the five attitudes toward singleness described in this chapter, which one do you most identify with?
2. Do you still look for someone to give you permission to try new things?
3. Name your top three priorities at the present time.
4. Describe a serendipity that happened to you recently.
5. Describe a serendipity that you were able to give to someone else in the past year.

12

New Pathways: Remarriage

The couple smiled warmly at me as I pronounced them man and wife. They embraced and then moved slowly to where the unity candle was waiting to be lighted. They looked at each other through the eyes of love as they lifted their candles toward the solitary unlighted candle. It lit, and they blew theirs out and returned it to the stand. As they moved back toward me, I invited their children to join them for prayer at the altar as we concluded the ceremony.

O God, we thank You for the vows of marriage that have been shared at this altar today. Now, as these children join hands in a circle of prayer with their parents, we ask Your blessing upon the blending of these two families into one unit.

Lord, we know that this union will perhaps be the most difficult of all. It will take time, great portions of patience, generous amounts of love, and the wisdom of gentle discipline.

O God, guide this new family unit as they share the joys and struggles of life in this adventure in love. Amen.

This was the conclusion to one of the many remarriage ceremonies I perform each year. It was not just a union of two people. It was a joining together of two families. The bridegroom had three children by a former marriage. The bride had two children. Now they both had five and would be living in the same house after the honeymoon.

After the ceremony, my mind drifted back a few years to the time when both of these single-again people joined one of my divorce-recovery classes. Both were coming out of ugly and demeaning divorces. Each questioned the chances of survival. The man took the time to tell me, after our re-marriage section of the seminar, that any thought of ever re-marrying was not a part of his agenda. Bitterness, hurt, anger, and guilt were a part of each of them. Now, almost two years later, life was introducing them to a new beginning.

Guidance Toward Remarriage

Seeing people remarry is one of my rewards for working with wounded lives. Meeting a person on the threshold of his or her hurt and seeing him move through the struggles of divorce and into a new life filled with hope and optimism is a big victory in a single-again ministry.

Before you run out and order your wedding invitations and book the local chapel, let's go back a way and examine the pathway that leads to the altar of remarriage.

The Reality of Remarriage

I would say that 90 percent of all the single-again people I meet would marry again if they could find the right person. I am frequently asked by some women, "Where are all the men my age?" The men stop me and ask where all the good women are hiding. Both seem to pass each other in the dark of night and continue their search.

The opportunities for remarriage for single-again people in their twenties and thirties are much greater than for those in their forties, fifties, and sixties. A quick visit to the three largest singles groups in your city will quickly let you know what the ratio of women to men is. If you look closely, you will find a very large membership of women over forty and a very small group of men the same age.

There are several reasons for the imbalance. First, men tend to be more vocational and recreational in their interests and life-styles; women tend more toward the relational. Men go to work in the morning; women go to meetings and events with other women. Men tend to be more guarded in the sharing of their struggles and feelings; women are more open and used to sharing their feelings. Men can initiate a new relationship while women stand around and wait to be asked. Men are taught to be resourceful and solve their own problems in life; women talk to other women and try to get help with their frustrations. A man will resist going to a counselor for help for fear of being unmasked and endangering his male image and ego. A woman more readily turns to any counseling help that is available and is more open and receptive to help.

I have watched men walk into a singles meeting, do a quick tally of the number of women versus the number of men, and make a speedy exit. No man in his right mind wants to join a women's group. He would rather be on the golf course or working alone in his garage on a hobby.

Another reality in the world of remarriage is that men tend to date women ten to twelve years younger than they are once they get past thirty-five or forty. A group of women from our forties class came to me one Sunday morning and asked permission to go and raid the thirties class and get all the forty-year-old men back. We laughed about it, but the sting of truth was there. It may not be fair, but it is a reality. I have asked some men how they feel about this. A few admitted that dating younger women makes them feel good. It bolsters their ego and helps them feel young. It sort of says, "Look what I have!"

From an older woman's standpoint, it can become a reminder that aging seems to work against women and for men.

What happens when an older man marries a younger woman? I will never forget a counseling session I had with a couple a number of years ago. It was one of those May-December unions, and it did not appear to be working out. I remember the strong comments from the woman as I gently explored the problem. It seemed to her that everything she wanted to buy or do brought one comment from her new husband: "I've already done that!" He had little interest in the things she wanted to do and explore in life because he had lived longer and done all those things. He simply wanted to settle down, take his young wife out for public viewing periodically, and then go home and smoke his pipe by the fireplace. This situation highlights one of the grave dangers of the spring-winter relationships. One person is an explorer and one is a settler. The tension of this kind of relationship can cause a speedy second divorce.

Steve had been single for twelve years. He was handsome, articulate, and a successful businessman. When I asked him jokingly why he hadn't latched onto one of the sweet young ladies in the singles group, he looked at me intently and said he was looking for a relationship but wanted it to be with someone his own age. He explained that he wanted someone who was on his level of life experientially. He added that he was looking for maturity in a woman, not just youthful attractiveness. Several years later when he married again, he married a woman only one year younger than himself. They are still married today!

Caution Signs in the Pathway to Remarriage

A woman approached me at the coffee break during a singles seminar. The question she asked might be rolling around in your mind right now: "How long should a person wait after her divorce is final before she starts dating again?" It is a commonly asked question. Another version of it goes like this: "How long should you wait to start dating again if your husband or wife has just left you?" I wish I could give a long list of recommended times for different situations, but I don't have enough paper for that. However, there are a few guidelines that apply to every single-again person who wrestles with this question:

Rule one. Don't start dating until you are emotionally ready for a new relationship in your life. Dates have a way of developing into a deeper relationship. You can really fall for a person on the first date. Your heartstrings may give the go signal, but your emotions may have you on hold.

Rule two. Don't start dating until you have stopped talking about your ex-spouse and telling all your divorce-war stories. No one wants to spend an evening being regaled with stories of how bad it was and how terrible it is. If you are still talking and thinking divorce, stay home.

Rule three. Don't date just to prove to yourself and your ex-spouse that you can get a date. If you are a woman and your ex has run off with a pretty young secretary, you may find yourself wanting to prove something.

I remember the lady who told me that her way to get back at her husband was to sleep with as many men as she could. She had been faithful all during her marriage, but when she found out he was having an affair, she decided to get even. For two years after the divorce, she jumped from bed to bed. She finally woke up and realized she was playing a losing game. She did not have to prove anything.

Rule four. Don't date just to relieve your loneliness. You may fill an evening, but you won't solve the problem.

Rule five. Date because you want to enjoy the company of other people. Don't be afraid to share emotional honesty with your date. Be yourself, and enjoy the experience. Always remember, no one is so cool that they don't falter and sputter in a few places. Feel free to laugh at yourself.

Rule six. Don't take your memory file along when you go on a date. Sitting in a restaurant and telling your date that you and your ex spent meaningful moments there will not get you high ratings in your date's mind.

Rule seven. Dating again after many years of marriage may make you feel like an adolescent again. Accept it and don't worry about it. Adolescents don't worry too much about tomorrow; they enjoy today. You should try to do the same.

Rule eight. (I may get into trouble here!) If you are a woman, I believe it is all right to ask a man out once in a while. I believe that men like to be asked every so often, instead of always having to do the asking. If you experience rejection, you will know how the last man you rejected felt.

Taking Your Time

We live in a world of microwave relationships. In other words, many people want a quick return on the investment of their time with another person. Some want to be paid with sexual involvement. Others want to be paid with a marriage ceremony.

I can recall the many phone conversations over the years that started like this:

"Jim, this is Bill Smith. Are you free on Saturday, the tenth of June, at three in the afternoon?"

"Yes, Bill, I'm free. What did you have in mind?"

"Jean and I want to get married, and we would like you to perform the ceremony."

"I didn't know you two were that serious!"

"Well, it's not the quantity of time, it's the quality."

"How long have you been going together?"

"Two months, but we are really in love!"

Does that sound familiar to you? When I ask people like Bill and Jean to take their time, they get offended and usually call someone else who can use fifty dollars for a quick tying of the marriage knot. Hurrying a new relationship to the altar can short-circuit it and leave you wondering what happened.

Over the past ten years, I have seen many second marriages end in divorce because the people involved did not give the relationship time to grow. My rule of thumb is that a new relationship takes from twelve to eighteen months to grow before it's ready for the altar. I applaud the people who take their time. There is much more to a second marriage than setting the date and walking down the aisle.

Getting to know your new love's children takes time. A second marriage does not create instant family. It just puts everyone under the same roof. Becoming a family takes time before the wedding and more time after the wedding. Instant adjustments seldom happen.

One friend of mine kept her new romance under wraps. When it was time to set the wedding date, she brought her new man home and simply announced to her three children that this was to be their new daddy. They all stood looking at him with their mouths open. They had only met him briefly once before, and now he was coming into their lives forever. Their shock, negative reaction, and stiff resistance kept the relationship on ice for a number of months to come.

It takes time and many different circumstances for your feelings for the children of another person to grow into love. They need as much, if not more, time to feel comfortable with you.

I have watched unhappy children ruin second marriages. I have seen them pit parent against stepparent in a contest that no one wins. As you build a new relationship with another person, take time and share love with his or her children.

Getting to know and love his or her family takes as much time as warming up to the children. Remarriage is inheriting instant in-laws and relatives. Some will approve of your new union, and some will not. You may find yourself locked in the struggle of trying to win their approval, regardless of the cost. Try to let those new relationships grow gradually. It is difficult to crash into the middle of someone's life and receive instant acceptance. Just because they are your new mate's family and you love him or her does not mean they will love you. Learn to spend time with all of them *before* you get married. Let them know you as you really are. Acceptance and love can never be forced.

Rejoining the Married Community

In the premarital counseling session I was conducting, the woman began to cry. When I asked what the problem was, she remarked on how sad she was to be leaving her singles group and moving back into the married group. She added that the singles had become her family after her divorce, and had walked through many battles and struggles with her over the past three years. Now she was changing communities again, and she wondered how she would be received as a "remarried" in the world of the "still marrieds."

Several years ago, three remarried couples came to me in a church I was serving and asked to start their own Sunday education class. They commented that they had tried several married classes but felt that they just didn't fit. Since they had special needs and struggles, they wanted their own group. We started a new class for them and called it the "Illuminators." Within a year's time, the class had over thirty couples, all of whom had entered the realm of remarriage. This is one creative way to handle the problem of reentry into the married world.

Some remarrieds have shared with me that they were made to feel like second-class citizens as they attempted to move back into the married community. Few people seemed to understand what they had gone through or even what they still had to go through as remarrieds. Sometimes patiently sharing your journey with others who haven't been there helps. At other times, you simply have to find those who have been there and begin rebuilding with their help.

One lady told me recently that her biggest problem in remarriage was meeting other marrieds who seemed to enjoy reminding her that she had been married before. She told me she resented being reminded of her scars. The people around you will not always be understanding. Some can be very cruel. You will eventually learn to smile at the time-worn comments and jabs directed at you and continue to build your life.

A New Pathway

Remarriage is vastly different from a first marriage. It is more complicated and demanding in every area. It takes hard work to make it happen. More second marriages fail than first marriages. Many people will choose it and make it work. Others will find themselves in a second divorce.

Making a second marriage work will mean asking God for all the help He can give you. God is in the rehabilitation business. He helps people start over again. He gives the strength and wisdom to make second marriages grow.

There are many bumps in this new pathway. Take your time to navigate carefully, ask your friends for help, and trust God to give you a new beginning for your life.

Personal-Growth Questions

(For best results, work with a small group
or one other person.)

1. What things still have to happen in your life before you will be ready for remarriage?
2. What are your greatest fears about remarriage?
3. How do you think God feels about remarriage?
4. How does the thought of never remarrying make you feel?
5. How do you feel about a woman asking a man out?
6. How long do you feel you should know a person before you consider remarriage?

13

Forgiveness: God's Detergent

As the middle-aged woman rose to leave my office, she turned and looked at me with tears running down her cheeks and said, "How can I ever forgive myself for what I've done? I feel so guilty!" I have lost track of how many times I have heard similar expressions from single-again people. Most of them get very specific and talk about the situations that are binding them with guilt. Some fear that there is no release from the guilt they feel as a result of the things they have done. To a few, it becomes a haunting feeling that they are never able to resolve.

The usual scenario on the guilt route goes something like this: You start thinking about a situation that happened in the past. You reflect on its negative outcome in your life and wonder if things would have been different had your responses in the situation been different. The "If I'd only" game I talked about earlier comes into focus. The "If I'd only" thoughts take over in your mind. As you begin to get buried in yesterday's memories, you start to feel guilty. You wish you could change it all or merely forget it forever.

Life is a series of choices, and all of us make some bad

169

ones. We choose the wrong mate, move to the wrong city, go to the wrong college, move into the wrong vocation, and end up feeling guilty for our choices. In an earlier chapter, I talked about the freedom to fail. If that kind of freedom is to be a part of our growth, we cannot afford to feel guilty when we fail in an area. The failure or the wrong decision should become a teaching experience and not a guilt box that closes us off from further growth.

Guilt in Divorce

There are three primary areas of guilt feelings associated with the divorce process. In talking with hundreds of people in divorce-recovery workshops, these three keep coming up:

1. *Inadequacies.* When things go wrong in our lives, we jump on the teeter-totter of BLAME. We tip the balance one way and place all the blame for what happened on the other person. Perhaps we meet someone who tells us that we were involved, also. Then we tip the balance the other way and assume all the blame ourselves. This inevitably results in the development of a martyr complex, a self-pity syndrome, and a great bout of depression. There is a subtle area that falls in between the two. We can blame outside people and outside forces and admit to our own powerlessness. Doing this makes us look good and the world look all wrong.

Dealing with your own inadequacies is simply being honest enough with yourself to admit you don't have all the answers. There is no one who is adequate in every situation. I meet many people who feel if they just read one more self-improvement book they will become adequate in all areas of life. It is simply not going to happen. Accepting your inadequacies is accepting your humanity. God did not create you to be a robot or a computer. You are a person, with all the human strengths and weaknesses.

I listen to long lists of inadequacies that people share with me as they go through a divorce. They feel they are inadequate in love, parenting, personality, patience, understanding, wisdom, empathy, kindness, ambition, sensitivity, and so on. Your list might be a lot longer. After you write them all down, I would ask you, "So what?" Are you going to merely admit to them and then run and hide behind them as an excuse not to deal with life? Or are you ready to tackle improving some of those areas that you know you need help with? Reality would perhaps be shouting out loud, "I blew it!" and then getting on with the rest of your life and learning how not to blow it as badly in the future.

2. Indecisions. I meet many single-again people who have a terrible time making up their minds. Their future is often on hold because they can't decide what to do. Others blame their divorce on their indecisions during their marriage. We are all indecisive at times. We feel that way because we don't want to make a wrong decision, so we often make no decision.

Yesterday's indecisive patterns can prohibit you from making the choices you need to make today. None of us can indict ourselves for yesterday's lack of decision making. That becomes another "If I'd only." It cannot be changed by feeling guilty about it. If your nature is still to be indecisive, I would suggest you get some help from a counselor or friend in decision making.

One of the most common indecisions I hear from divorced people is, "I wish we had gone to a counselor or marriage specialist in time to prevent this divorce." The reality is, by the time you acknowledge this, it's too late to do anything about it. Hindsight is only valuable as a teacher for today.

The indecisions of yesterday can cause a form of guilt from which there is no release. They keep your mind in reverse and seldom allow you to deal with the decisions of today. Forget the decisions you wish you had made. Get on with the ones you can make right now.

3. *Decisions.* When was the last time you made a quick decision and regretted it later? Sometimes it seems to happen at least once or twice a day. You get in the line for movie tickets that seems to be moving the fastest, and it stalls. The other lines sail by you, and you continue to wait. Wrong decision! You get into what seems to be the faster-moving lane on the highway, only to find yourself in a traffic jam. Wrong decision!

Life can fill up pretty fast with wrong decisions. Too many of these will send you running from any kind of decision-making process. You can start piling up a mountain of guilt over the decisions you have made that turned out badly.

When you go through a divorce, you are reminded of the decision you made back down the road to get married. Now that you are at the point of divorce, it seems you made the wrong choice. As you look around at people who are still married, it seems as though they made the right choice. You are wrong, they are right, and the guilt starts to sweep over you.

All of us make decisions based on information and emotion. Sometimes we have too little, other times too much. Life is deciding. Decisions made are decisions filed and lessons learned. You can't undo them. You can't run from them. You have to live with them.

Guilt Over Death

After the funeral I was leading, the widow came over and thanked me for the memorial service. As she was about to walk away, she said, "If only I had made John take better care of himself, he would be alive today!" Her feelings, if entertained very long, could bring about a deep sense of guilt over her husband's death. Many people who lose a mate by death feel that they could have done something to prevent it from happening, but they didn't. Guilt feelings over not doing certain things can cling to a person for a long time.

Death is so final that you cannot even offer an apology for something you felt you did wrong. It seems there is no place to deal with any guilt that arises after death. The best resolution to this is to realize that you really did the best you knew how. Again, hindsight is only of value as we reflect it toward the pathway ahead of us.

Anger is another emotion that is often felt after the death of a mate. One man said to me, "How could my wife just go and die on me and leave me with four children? I am so angry at her for leaving me with all this responsibility." The waves of emotion at being left alone in life are difficult to calm. Each day alone causes the anger to increase. Guilt at feeling angry only adds to the confusion.

Your life plan is always messed up when someone dies. Anger and guilt have to be recognized, expressed, and dealt with. They are honest feelings. Talk them out with trusted friends, and you will find a beginning sense of relief about them. Slowly readjust your focus from the corridors of yesterday to the stairway of today.

The Way Out of Guilt

I believe that one of the best tools God has given us to handle guilt is forgiveness. Guilt always adds to more guilt. Forgiveness sets us free from guilt.

I was about six years of age when I decided to become a cookie thief. Mom has just baked some of her chocolate-chip specials. I was going through the kitchen and out to play in our yard when I decided to pilfer a few without Mom's permission. About an hour later, I was called in from play and asked if I had taken any cookies. After a thorough grilling by my mother, I admitted to the theft. (It was pretty obvious, since I was the only other person at home.) Mom sent me to the confinement of my room for the next two hours as punishment. Those were the days when a boy's bedroom was not a haven full of various entertaining electronic equipment.

After two hours of boredom, I was released. But a strange thing happened. I had served my time, but I wasn't sure I was really forgiven. I hung around the house with a pouting attitude until my mom patted me on the head and assured me everything was all right and I could go outside to play. Those pats on the head were what I needed. They meant I was *really* forgiven, and any guilt I still felt was removed. I was free to move on with my life without a permanent blot on my record.

Forgiveness is really God's detergent to make us whole again. In 1 John 1:9, we see the heart of God embodied in the forgiveness process. It says, "If we confess our sins, he is faithful and just, and will forgive our sins and cleanse us from all unrighteousness."

Confession brings cleansing and forgiveness. The cleansing and forgiveness are wonderful. The confession is extremely difficult. Confession is an admission of our inability to do everything right. It admits our humanity, our weakness, our imperfection. It admits to wrong decisions, indecisions, anger, and guilt. Confession is saying, "I blew it and I'm sorry." It is taking the blame ourselves.

Accepting God's promise of forgiveness means that I have to forgive others as well. It was Peter who asked Jesus how many times one should forgive another person. Peter was quick to ask if 7 times was enough. Jesus' response was 70 times 7. What He really meant was not 490 times, but an unlimited number of times.

I am sure that many men and women would like to do their weekly laundry just once and have it last for the rest of their lives. The problem is that the clothes worn by the family keep getting dirty and need to be washed. It is a neverending chore.

In a way, we are like that laundry pile. We get pretty scruffy from life's situations. We need a constant application of God's finest detergent: forgiveness!

Maybe your prayer right now would look something like this:

God, forgive me for the things I feel guilty about not doing. Forgive me for the things I feel guilty about doing. I confess to You my inadequacies and accept Your continuous promise of forgiveness. Amen.

Recently I spoke to a large group of singles about forgiveness. During the question period, a lady asked to share a few thoughts from her own experience regarding forgiveness. She told us she and her ex-spouse were bitter enemies and had had little communication since their divorce. She had struggled with not being able to ask him for forgiveness. Finally, she took the risk, went to him, and asked him to forgive her for the things she knowingly and unknowingly had done wrong that contributed to their marriage failure. He forgave her and also asked her to forgive him in the same light. Her comment to the group about this experience was, "It seemed as though all the hate, hurt, anger, and guilt just evaporated the moment forgiveness was enacted. I have never felt better and more relieved of a burden in my whole life. Forgiveness works!"

In my desk I have a file of letters that contain similar accounts. Forgiveness is really God's ultimate guilt remover. It sets us free to go on with our lives. It releases us from having to try to be perfect, and lets us simply be human. It settles accounts with other people that often load us with guilt.

Jesus personified ultimate forgiveness on the cross when He uttered the words, "Father, forgive them; for they know not what they do" (Luke 23:34). Sometimes we don't really know what we are doing, either. We need God's forgiveness, and we need the forgiveness of others. We will be free from guilt in our lives when we exercise God's provision of forgiveness!

Personal-Growth Questions

(For best results, work with a small group
or one other person.)

1. How do you usually handle things that make you feel guilty?
2. How much guilt are you assuming for your present single-again status?
3. Describe an experience in which your guilt disappeared when you claimed forgiveness?
4. Are you living with an experience in which you desire forgiveness but don't feel you have it?
5. How easy or difficult is it for you to forgive another person?

14

Being Me and Growing Free

Many suddenly single-again people choose to live at the point of their death or divorce crisis far too long. A crisis impedes growth. It provides an excuse for those who want to hide and not face new beginnings. It becomes a convenient cocoon in which to harbor the past and hinder the future. Life goes on, and you must go on. Growing free of a crisis starts when you are willing to enter the emergency room of life and begin treatment. The mourning and grieving that are a natural process come to an end when you are willing to start new growth.

Repairing Your Wounds

If I put my hand through a window in my house and receive a six-inch cut, I race off to the local hospital and book myself a room for the next six months. No! I go to the emergency room of that hospital and ask if I can have my wound stitched up. Usually, in the space of an hour or so, I am free to return home, wound bandaged, but ready to repair the window I just broke. My progress will be impaired, and I may even have some pain, but I go about my day and my tasks as before.

Receiving help is always a part of the healing process. Many people are simply too proud or too afraid to ask for some help in the healing of their hurts. There are caring people who will give their hands and hearts when someone goes through a divorce or death crisis. As that pain subsides, new pains come along. Loneliness, fear of the future, self-doubt, loss of friends, and indecision are some of these.

The beginning of a new life is a frightening experience. Several people have shared with me that their divorce was like an operation. It took a while to recover from the surgery, but they felt that they were taking weekly trips to the hospital for further repairs. There seemed to be so many things the surgery failed to resolve. Some of those repairs involve inner healing of the spirit, while others involve the practical, everyday human needs we all have. Many single-again people feel that they should simply get well all of a sudden, and never need minor repairs again.

A newly divorced man told me he was going to have a T-shirt printed up with the slogan "Temporarily out of commission." He wanted to wear it on the days when things were rocky, and he needed some outside help in his life.

Do you feel free enough to go to the emergency room once in a while for some help? Maybe it's just an emotional lift that you need from a friend: a solid word of encouragement—an affirmation—an idea. At other times it may mean going to a professional counselor or therapist. It doesn't mean you are doing poorly. It means that you are choosing to do better. Don't be afraid to ask for some help as your new journey unfolds.

Meeting Your Needs

As I have talked and counseled with single-again people across the country, they have shared five basic needs that they are working on meeting in their lives. These five needs become the basis for solid growth in single living. As I share them, do a mental checkup and see how you are doing.

Relational needs. In an earlier chapter, I talked about building relationships. I dealt with the personal side of the one-to-one relationships we all need. Along with the personal, we need the supportive group of friends that forms a community for us. Because many single-again people lose their married-community support systems, it is important to build a new system that will add meaning and continuity to life. One of the fastest-growing new ministries in churches across America is the ministry to single adults. Many churches have over five hundred singles in their programs.

The church-oriented singles community provides an ideal place for single-again people to meet new friends and build strong new relationships. The church group also offers an alternative to some of the secular singles groups that are known for their "search and seizure" agendas.

One of the most difficult meetings to go to for the first time is a singles meeting. The media have not been too kind in describing singles and singles activities. Some singles complain that groups are filled with "losers." I always get a little defensive when I hear that. I am not sure why being single is supposed to be synonymous with being a loser. The singles I meet are winners, not losers.

Most people fear going to an activity where they don't know anyone else. They wonder if they will be accepted, if the people will be friendly, if the program will be interesting. Perhaps an even greater concern is finding someone with whom they might be interested in pursuing a relationship. These are human needs and human feelings, and they are part of reaching out to a new group.

Single-again people quickly discover that it is no fun doing things alone. A singles group provides the opportunity to do things in community. Fun and joy are shared experiences. A singles group provides support when you are struggling with those new beginnings. The people in it become fellow strugglers. You have the knowledge that you are not alone.

Most people do two things with group experiences: They choose to either isolate themselves from, or to relate to, a group. Those in isolation seldom grow and often are buried in loneliness and self-pity. Those who reach out find community and caring, and are also able to provide that for others. It is comforting to know that others have problems, too. Mutual strength and support come from shared lives.

I get letters from many singles asking how to find a singles group in their area. Few singles find a group to join on their first attempt. Usually you have to visit several groups before you find one that you feel comfortable in. A good indicator of the quality of a group is seeing the following things happening:

1. Lots of laughing, hugging, and a general warm spirit.
2. A well-planned and executed program.

3. A friendly welcome to first-time attenders.
4. Good literature telling about upcoming events.
5. A good mix of both men and women in the group.
6. The people directing the program are alive and sparkling.
7. You get a call or letter after your visit asking how you liked the meeting and inviting you to the next function.

Don't get discouraged in your search for a good singles community. Many singles try one group, get discouraged, and judge all others by that group. Take the time to make your rounds. It can be as important in your life as finding a dentist, doctor, or car mechanic.

Another word of caution: You can get worn out in a group. Being overworked in positions of responsibility with little thanks can send you running for cover. You may need to take it easy once in a while and rest in the back row, while the group ministers to you. Always give your group a chance to love you, and love them in return. The more society, through technology and mechanization, drives people from each other, the stronger our need for grouping will become. Find a group to help you grow!

Social needs. When you ask a single person how his or her social life is, they might respond by saying that they are not dating anyone right now. That is a part of one's social existence, but it doesn't mean your life is the pits due to a lack of a special someone. I define social life as the fun things I do with other people. Married people tend to do social things with each other or with other married friends. Many single-again people allow their social lives to fall into ruin because they cannot envision themselves having fun with people other than the ones they once associated with.

Building a new social existence as a newly single person involves trying some things you have never done before. New social adventures can put excitement back into your life. Make a list of some of the things you would like to try: skydiving—learning to fly—skiing—taking music lessons—rafting on the river—hiking in the wilderness. Don't be stopped by the tape in your mind that says, "I never did that before." I vividly remember the quiet little lady in one of our singles groups who was always organizing backpacking trips. She was well over sixty, and more feminine than muscular. Yet, she was the first to shoulder her backpack and head out on the trail each morning. When everyone else was dying of exhaustion, she was over the rim of the next hill. It was an entirely new hobby she took up after her husband died. Discovering new hobbies that you can share with others in your singles group will help you grow socially.

Spiritual needs. In the course of counseling appointments, I sometimes ask single people how they are doing in the spiritual areas of their lives. Some respond by telling me they go to church, read their Bible occasionally, pray for their food before meals, and even tell somebody what they believe about God once in a while. For many, that appears to be the spiritual growth checklist. If they are doing all of them, they must be growing. The truth is that they can simply be following mechanical rituals that have no effect on their daily lives.

Spiritual growth is building a relationship with God. It is being sensitive to what He would want in our lives. It is getting directions from Him in the daily decisions we are confronted with. This kind of growth takes time and often is not open for public inspection. It involves the same process we go through in building relationships with other human beings. Spiritual growth is walking with God through all the situations of life, believing His promises and knowing that He loves us.

We relate to God on a one-to-one basis in our spiritual growth. We also relate to God through our Christian friends. They provide a spiritual climate and community of love in which our growth can thrive.

Are you growing in your relationship with God? Do you have friends to grow with you? Do you belong to a church that enables you to grow?

Educational needs. Reaching out for your fullest human potential is an educational process. Many singles take academic courses in local colleges that will further their careers and improve the salary on their jobs. On-the-job training programs are a part of continuing education. All this is important to building self-worth and self-esteem. But if it is the only educational program you have for yourself, you will fall short on the personal-growth level. Along with the outside growth, there has to be something taking place on the inside of your life. Here is a list for you to reflect on as you consider some interior redesigning in your life:

1. How am I doing in expressing and handling my feelings and emotions?

2. Am I acting on situations in my life or reacting to those situations?

3. Am I learning to assert myself in dealing with others, or am I constantly being manipulated and intimidated?

4. Do I feel good about myself and believe that I am worth something as a person?

5. Am I making significant and important changes in my personality?

6. Do I have direction in my life, or am I letting others direct me?

7. Are my feelings of self-confidence growing? Do I increasingly believe in myself and my abilities?

That's a short list. You can probably add several more items after you get started.

There are numerous good books in the self-help category that can assist your growth in any of these areas. (*See* the reading list at the end of the book.) Local schools offer courses in the evening designed to help you grow and become a more confident person. The opportunities are there for you. Don't sit numbly. Pick out the area you need help in and get it!

Emotional needs. In ten years of working with thousands of single-again people, I have watched many coming to one of my groups for the first time. Some are so emotionally tired and overloaded with their problems that even their physical appearance is stooped. Conversing with them only verifies their emotional battles.

In divorce-recovery seminars, I tell people that the divorce war is generally waged on two fronts: the practical and the emotional. For most people, the emotional is far more difficult than the practical.

First of all, your emotions tend to yo-yo on you. Just when you have one set of feelings lined up, something happens to send them reeling off in another direction. The feelings of love and hate toward a former spouse are a good example of this. Several months after a separation or divorce, you see your ex-spouse in a store. You don't know whether you should run over and embrace him or her and tell him how badly you have missed him, or whether you should mash him against the shelves with your shopping cart. At best, you have feelings of ambivalence.

Memories have a way of hooking you emotionally. You think you have filed and cataloged them from your mind. A word or a picture instantly brings them back into view, and you may be upset for the rest of the day.

Emotions cannot be denied. They have to be sorted out, expressed, and dealt with. You either express them or repress them. When repressed, they often explode upon you when you least expect them, like a well-shaken bottle of soda. Some single adults suffer from emotional whiplash. It's being hit from behind by emotional problems you thought were taken care of but in reality were simply ignored.

There are several positive things you can do in resolving and rebuilding emotional structures:

1. Don't lock yourself away with your emotions. Find a few very trusted friends to share them with. Emotions

are tied to your feelings, and feelings are neither right nor wrong. They just are.

2. Find ways to express your emotions. Verbalizing is one way. Writing them down in the form of a journal or diary is another. Thinking them through in moments of quiet meditation and reflection is yet another. Emotions have a way of piling up on each other. It is hard to sort them out when they become entangled.

3. Recognize where your emotions are right now. If you know where you are, you will know where to head. Having someone tell you that you should not feel the way you do will not resolve the emotion. It will just hang a cloud of guilt over you.

4. Make some positive plans that will help get your emotions under control. Maybe getting out of the heat of your present situation for a time will give you a release. Try a few days away, a short vacation. You need time to get a broader perspective.

Our emotional structures are a part of our lives. They either run unchecked and out of control, or we own them and decide to be responsible for them. We can feel high or low emotionally. Situations can direct our emotions, or we can take charge of the situations and our emotions. Growing emotionally will help you feel good about yourself.

My Healing Goes On

In John 5:9, we read about the end of one part of a man's life and the beginning of another part. The verse says, "At once the man recovered, picked up his bed and began to walk" (PHILLIPS). In reading back over the biblical account, we see a man who was brought to the crossroads of a new beginning. His change of direction was brought about by a healing miracle. Physically he became well. But that is only part of his story. The writer tells us that his journey was not over. It says he *"began* to walk." That tells us that the second half of his healing was a process.

Divorce and death are not events. They are processes that are walked through and lived out. The healing for the man involved a new direction. In that new direction there was a learning process, and it could not be speeded up. Many single-again people are in a hurry to get on down the road. They look for the quickest and easiest answers to their struggles. Be aware that the quick answers are, at best, Band-Aids. They seldom go to the heart of the matter.

All healing takes time. Beginning to walk says that a person might fall and stumble a bit, or even slide backward. When a small child attempts to take his first steps and falls midway across the three-foot distance to his parents' outstretched arms, he is not spanked and placed in his crib and told he will never be able to walk. He is promptly dusted off, placed with one parent, and shoved off again. This is done repeatedly until the child walks the distance. And it's not over when the three feet are spanned. Then it's stretched to six feet, nine feet, and all the way across the room. Stumbling, falling, starting over. It is all a part of walking. Beginning to walk says . . .

> . . . there will be good days and bad days
> . . . there will be setbacks and advances

> ... there will be tears and laughter
> ... there will be hurts and healings.

Right after the man in the Scriptures began his new journey, he was verbally attacked by those who could not affirm his healing and wanted to attack the healer. Sometimes when you are being healed and are getting well, you make those around you nervous and jealous. Perhaps their growth is not going as well as yours. Instead of asking for your help in their process, they become critical and envious of your healing. Don't let critical voices slow your healing. You may have to turn a deaf ear in their direction and continue on your course. Healing life's hurts is a slow process. The greatest gift you can give yourself is the gift of time. God is never in a hurry. His working time is from eternity to eternity.

Personal-Growth Questions

(For best results, work with a small group
or one other person.)

1. Describe how you feel your current relational needs are being met or not being met.
2. How has your social life changed since you became single again?
3. Describe how you feel you are doing in the area of emotional growth.
4. How far along do you feel you are in your own healing-of-hurts process?
5. What are your feelings when you go to singles functions where you have never been before?

A Final Word

Thousands of single-again people have shared the journey you have taken in these pages. Undoubtedly, your life will be different as a result. There are no easy answers to the suddenly single-again experience. Most of the victories are hard won. Inevitable scars will remain to remind you of your journey. They are signposts of the journey and badges of growth to the bearer.

You have read this book, and now you can draw your own conclusions. The challenge to get on with your life rests in your hands.

My prayer is that God will grant you the wisdom to make the right choices and the patience to let those choices become crystal clear to you.

You are suddenly single again—but you are not alone!

Recommended Reading

Augsburger, David. *Caring Enough to Forgive.* Ventura, Calif.: Regal Books, 1981.

Barkas, J. L. *Single in America.* New York: Atheneum, 1980.

Conway, Jim. *Men in Mid-Life Crisis.* Elgin, Ill.: Cook, 1978.

Gould, Roger L. *Transformations: Growth and Change in Adult Life.* New York: Touchstone Books, 1979.

Juroe, David J. *Money: How to Spend Less and Have More.* Old Tappan, N. J.: Fleming H. Revell Company, 1981.

Richards, Larry. *Remarriage: A Healing Gift From God.* Waco, Tex.: Word, Inc., 1981.

Sheehy, Gail. *Pathfinders.* New York: William Morrow and Company, Inc., 1981.

Small, Dwight. *Christian: Celebrate Your Sexuality.* Old Tappan, N. J.: Fleming H. Revell Company, 1974.

———. *How Should I Love You?* New York: Harper and Row Publishers, Inc., 1979.

Smoke, Jim. *Growing Through Divorce.* Eugene, Oreg.: Harvest House Publishers, Inc., 1976.